BRI

MRS. DALLOWAY AND TO THE LIGHTHOUSE BY VIRGINIA WOOLF

Intelligent Education

Nashville, Tennessee

BRIGHT NOTES: Mrs. Dalloway and To the Lighthouse
www.BrightNotes.com

ISBN: 978-1-645425-26-7 (Paperback)
ISBN: 978-1-645425-27-4 (eBook)

Originally published by Monarch Press.
Martin D. Levenson, 1966
2020 Edition published by Influence Publishers.

Interior design by Lapiz Digital Services. Cover Design by Thinkpen Designs.

Printed in the United States of America.

Library of Congress Cataloging-in-Publication Data forthcoming.
Names: Intelligent Education
Title: BRIGHT NOTES: Mrs. Dalloway and To the Lighthouse
Subject: STU004000 STUDY AIDS / Book Notes

CONTENTS

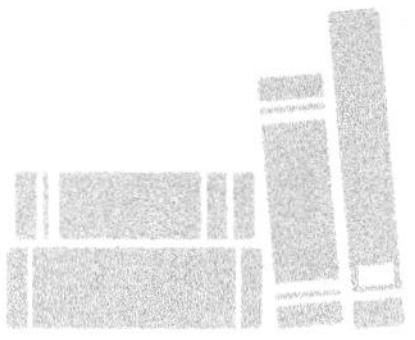

VIRGINIA WOOLF

INTRODUCTION

Virginia Woolf was born in 1882 into one of England's most distinguished literary families. Her father, Sir Leslie Stephen (whom she was later to portray as Mr. Ramsay in *To The Lighthouse*) was an editor (of the *Dictionary of National Biography* and the *Cornhill Magazine*), a critic, biographer and philosopher, a man who moved in the best Victorian literary circles. And his relatives - the Stephens - were most of them equally distinguished: his brother a jurist and Anglo-Indian administrator, his niece the Principal of Newnham College, etc. His first wife was Thackeray's daughter; his second - Julian Jackson - was a famous, an almost legendary, beauty (on whom Virginia Woolf, of course, based her portrait of Mrs. Ramsay). By her he had four children - Julian Thoby, Adrian, Vanessa and Virginia, and since she herself already had three children from an earlier marriage, the Stephen menage must indeed have closely resembled that of the Ramsays.

More important, with its vigorous intellectual atmosphere - Leslie Stephen, a typical Victorian parent in some respects (not allowing his daughters to smoke or go about unchaperoned, for instance) gave them the complete freedom of his large and unexpurgated library even in their early teens - this household provided the perfect nourishment for a developing writer. And perhaps most important of all, the social class to which Virginia Woolf belonged by virtue of her "Stephen connection" enabled her almost automatically to think of herself in professional terms, to think not - as some women would have to - of "scribbling," but of seriously writing and of being taken seriously. For the members of the Victorian "intellectual aristocracy," as Noel Annan (a biographer of Leslie Stephen has noted, had established almost a complete "intellectual ascendency" in their society, and they shared "the spoils of the professional and academic worlds among their children." If one belonged by birth to this literary "establishment" (and birth was probably a better passport to it than talent) "no very great merit was required" (and here Virginia Woolf herself is speaking) "to put you into a position where it was easier on the whole to be eminent than obscure."

Thus doors were opened easily, naturally, to Virginia Woolf. She had to spend little or no energy in knocking and beating at them. As a child, in her own drawing room she met - through her father - important literary figures like Henry James and James Russell Lowell. As a young girl she was introduced by her brother Thoby to the circle of talented young Cantabridgians who were eventually to be known as the Bloomsbury Group. As a grown woman she was herself at the center of this group, the very hub of the London literary wheel. In short, from first to last the atmosphere of literary England was her life-breath; there was no sudden adolescent "revelation" of a new and unfamiliar literary landscape as there is for so many writers. Instead the countryside - to extend the **metaphor** - was naturally, inevitably mapped out for her, full of familiar hamlets in which she'd been vacationing since the age of five. On the whole, such an intimate, family connection with literature - though it may narrow and rarify a writer's work (as it did to some extent with Virginia

Woolf) - can be a great boon to a writer, for his self-image is thus absolutely consistent, perfectly formed from an early age. There is no conflict between family expectations and his own artistic expectations, between family style and artistic style. He is free to concentrate - as a writer should be - entirely on his work.

BLOOMSBURY

After Sir Leslie Stephen died in 1904, his two daughters, Vanessa and Virginia, set up housekeeping with their brothers Thoby and Adrian at 46 Gordon Square, one of the Bloomsbury squares. To this house came a large group of friends, some of them Bloomsbury neighbors, others Thoby's classmates from Cambridge. When Thoby died in 1906 and Vanessa in 1907 married Clive Bell, Adrian and Virginia moved to nearby Fitzroy Square, but the same group continued to visit them. "The nucleus of the Bloomsbury Group," states Monique Nathan, "was a set of friends Thoby Stephen had made at Cambridge, where they had formed their own 'Midnight Society.' Chief among these apostles, as they called themselves, were Lytton Strachey, Clive Bell, and Leonard Woolf." Others included Duncan Grant, the artist, John Maynard Keynes, the economist, Desmond MacCarthy, the critic, and Roger Fry, E. M. Forster, J. Lowes Dickinson, T. S. Eliot. "Bloomsbury," as Monique Nathan depicts the group, "was not a sober and inexpensive residential quarter between New Oxford Street and High Holborn, but rather a state of mind. The state of mind was nonconformity in all things: a wholesome reaction against the boredom of fashionable life, and the expression of a real need for intellectual freedom."

Madame Nathan neglects to note, however, the central and all-pervasive influence on this group of Bloomsbury artists and thinkers of the Cambridge philosopher G. E. Moore, under whose spell Thoby and his friends had fallen while they were at the university. (Moore's *Principia Ethica,* his most important work, was published in 1903.) Moore believed, as K. W. Gransden summarizes it, that "the contemplation of beauty in art and the cultivation of personal relations were the most important things in life," and this philosophy influenced Virginia Woolf as much as her brother and his friends. Certainly her novels, more often than not, deal with the complex perfection of certain moments (and with their preservation in art); and certainly, too, the "cultivation" of personal relations was often her province as a novelist, rather than the larger social context against which personal relations are formed. She did, however, as we shall see, occasionally explore both the life of the mind and, in an admittedly subtle and delicate way, the structure of society, beyond the narrow limits of what came to be called Bloomsbury "aestheticism," an aestheticism which may be defined by Gransden's summary of Moore's central precepts.

FEMINISM

One definitely nonaesthetic concern of Virginia Woolf's - a social interest which persisted throughout her life - was her passionate feminism. Like most distinguished women, she felt that woman had for too long been subjugated-relegated to the kitchen, the nursery and the bedroom - and she often speculated on the subject of woman's innate abilities, which she was sure were equal to men's, despite the much lower level of female achievement in the arts and sciences. What might have happened to a twin sister of Shakespeare's, she once wondered, to a girl possessing all the poet's talents but denied the opportunities he was given - the education, the chance to go on the stage (for women couldn't act in Elizabethan theatres)? Is it not possible, Mrs. Woolf added, that such a girl, tormented by talent she could not express, may be buried in some unmarked grave, driven to suicide or crime or madness by her "differentness," her genius? In *A Room of One's Own* (1929) and *Three Guineas* (1938) Mrs. Woolf proposed her own solutions to the female problem-among them equal educational opportunities, leisure for self-cultivation, and new attitudes toward women. And though critics like Monique Nathan and Queenie Leavis have objected to the author's feminism-Madame Nathan Because it seems outdated, "a quaint relic of the Victorian era"; Mrs. Leavis because it seems unrealistic - she is still, in these books, one of the most articulate and persuasive spokesmen that the cause of "women's rights" has ever had. Indeed, her own accomplishments as a novelist themselves prove two of her basic points - that women may be just as talented as men, and that their environment and upbringing may often keep them from realizing their fullest potentiality. For much as Virginia Woolf achieved as a novelist, she was herself both aided and limited by her peculiarly feminine point of view.

THE FLIGHT FROM NATURALISM

Virginia Woolf has often been called a novelist of sensibility, an intensely feminine novelist. Three main forces seem to have shaped her into this kind of writer. First, of course, she was naturally poetic - that is, she had a poet's temperament - the eye for **metaphor** and **imagery**, the ear for language, the delight in style which more often characterizes lyric poets than novelists. Second, the sheltered thought vigorously intellectual life which she led as a result primarily of her sex (though to a lesser extent of her social class) tended to develop her sensibility, her feminine appreciation of subtle shades of thought and feeling, rather than a larger, more objective social consciousness. (Thus, as we noted above, she was both aided and limited by her femininity.) Finally, and perhaps most importantly, the objective naturalistic novel, the novel of social consciousness and dramatic fact, seemed at the point when Mrs. Woolf began writing seriously, to have gone about as far as it could go.

Writers like Hardy, George Moore, Arnold Bennett, Galsworthy, and even the young D. H. Lawrence had thoroughly explored the English class structure, the external reality of life; the trivial-seeming facts of innumerable personal histories; they had developed and extended in their work, in England, the sort of social **realism** (or "naturalism" as it was called in certain cases) which was first attempted by French writers like Flaubert, Balzac, Zola and Huysmans. Now the novel had to find a new field to explore; the old territory was exhausted. And what more logical than for writers in English like Joyce and Mrs. Woolf and Dorothy Richardson to turn inward, to turn-following now in the footsteps of the American Henry James as well as Frenchmen like the omnipresent Flaubert (who influenced everybody) and the obscure Dujardin-to the novel of subjectivity or, as Leon Edel calls it, the "psychological novel"? Whatever one calls it, this sort of novel-as we shall see in reading *Mrs. Dalloway* and *To the Lighthouse,* differs from the realistic novel in that its action is mainly internalized: the principal action takes place not in the real world of events, of marriages and catastrophes, but (though events, of course, do occur in such novels) in the mind, the all-absorbing "stream of consciousness." Thought, in other words, is event in the subjective novel, for thought includes - as, again, we shall see in *Mrs. Dalloway* and *To the Lighthouse* - not only crucial decisions and emotions but also the memories of real events.

EARLY NOVELS

Virginia Woolf did not, of course, begin writing experimental, subjective novels from the first; like most artists she had to evolve a distinctive style over a period of years-almost fifteen years, to be exact. She began writing her first novel, *The Voyage Out,* in 1909, when she was twenty-seven; she was already publishing book reviews at this point, though she was not to become known as a creative writer until this first book was published, six years later in 1915, several years after she had married Leonard Woolf. Though it quite clearly displayed much promise, *The Voyage Out* (in which Mr. and Mrs. Dalloway, interestingly enough, make a brief first appearance as characters) was significant mainly as a first novel by a talented novelist; even Mrs. Woolf's friend and admirer, Lytton Strachey, who read the book with "breathless pleasure" complained that it lacked "the cohesion of a dominating idea."

It was followed in 1919 by *Night and Day* and then, in 1922, by *Jacob's Room,* in which Mrs. Woolf for the first time seriously experimented with the traditional style and form of the novel. It was not till *Mrs. Dalloway,* however, (published in 1925), that she seemed to have completely understood the direction-toward greater subjectivity-in which her talent was leading her. *Jacob's Room,* despite its lyric intensity, is still technically uneven, not yet the work of a mature artist.

MRS. DALLOWAY AND TO THE LIGHTHOUSE

In contrast to *Jacob's Room, Mrs. Dalloway,* though it is not usually considered her best novel, is still Mrs. Woolf's best-known, most widely read and most frequently studied novel. Perhaps this is because in *Mrs. Dalloway,* for the first time, Virginia Woolf applied both subjectivist and, as W. Y. Tindall has noted, symbolist precepts to the novel-exploring the minds of her characters in all their flow and flux and yoking together two seemingly unrelated characters in a kind of extended **metaphysical** conceit, to produce not only one of the first psychological novels but also one of the first symbolist-metaphysical novels (cf. Introduction to *Mrs. Dalloway*), a work which may seem a bit strained and unnecessarily ambiguous to some readers but which is still historically significant.

To the Lighthouse, on the other hand, is not only widely read; it is also often spoken of (along with *The Waves*) as Mrs. Woolf's finest and most moving novel. Intenser than *Mrs. Dalloway* because more closely based on autobiographical fact, it has, as a result of its autobiographical origins, a poignant reality which reinforces its lyricism and its subjectivity to produce a three-dimensional record of life both as it is felt and as it is perceived.

ORLANDO, A PORTRAIT OF THE ARTIST AS A TIME MACHINE

After writing *To the Lighthouse,* Mrs. Woolf relaxed with the wonderful jeu d'esprit that is *Orlando.* At this point, fatigued by the intense concentration which her self-evolution as a novelist had demanded, she felt the need to feel free, to have fun writing a less "serious" novel. The "escapade," as she called it, turned out to be *Orlando,* the fantastic biography of an Englishman-woman (starting out as a man the hero is, significantly, transformed into a woman in the eighteenth century) which begins in the year 1500 and traces the life of its hero heroine through to "the present moment," October, 1928.

But *Orlando* is not only a fantastically long-lived character (one who lives at a different pace from the rest of the world, for he-she is only thirty-eight years old at the end of the novel, when five hundred years of normal time have passed); he-she is also a kind of embodiment of English literature, and of Mrs.

Woolf's own consciousness as it ranges over the history of five hundred years of western civilization. Literally, then, the book is a portrait of the artist as a time machine, a magical invention free to experience and comment on all time.

THE WAVES, THE NOVEL AS VERSE PLAY

The serious work which Virginia Woolf had already planned to succeed *Orlando* was indeed far more ambitious than its predecessor. In it the author traced the lives and relationships of six characters, setting the stages of their growth and age against the progress of sun and weather on a day at the beach; and in the terms of the novel the six characters are the waves which beat upon this symbolic shore-waves of consciousness which remind us that Mrs. Woolf had once likened Proust's characters to waves that move in the "sea of thought." What is perhaps most distinctive about *The Waves,* however, is not its use of the sea-imagery to which Virginia Woolf was so frequently attracted, but the particular style in which the story is told: a series of highly stylized, poetic monologues or soliloquies in which each character relates his perceptions and reactions - his "thought and comment and analysis" of the situation in which he finds himself. Thus Mrs. Woolf seems to have transformed the traditional form of the novel almost into a kind of verse play, a ritual narrative in which the participants confront themselves-in a sense purge themselves - through an incantatory record of experience and emotion.

THE LAST YEARS

Those critics who do not feel that *To the Lighthouse* is Mrs. Woolf's best-most moving and convincing-book, tend to award the honors to *The Waves*, which, with its poetic structure seems like an emanation of all that is most distinctively Woolfian. At any rate, by most critics, the last two books - *The Years* (1937) and *Between the Acts* (1941) are not considered up to Mrs. Woolf's earlier achievements (though this is rather less true of *Between the Acts*, which has some adherents who would rank it with the best of the earlier books). In this period Mrs. Woolf also did a good deal of nonfiction writing (she had, of course, been active as a book reviewer and essayist from the very beginning of her career). *The Common Reader: Second Series, Flush* (a fanciful biography of the Brownings' dog), *Three Guineas* (one of her feminist tracts) and *Roger Fry: A Biography* were all published after *The Waves* appeared-between 1932 and 1941, the year of the novelist's death.

THE FINAL GESTURE

Despite her productivity, the persistent elegance and merriment of her style, Mrs. Woolf still felt - as Clarissa Dalloway and Septimus Warren Smith had felt - an urge toward death. There were many external pressures on her, of course, most important of these the war (World War II), which horrified her as World War I had horrified Septimus (and his creator) so many years earlier. But the internal pressure, the pressure of a "recurrent mental illness" which as we have noted (cf. Introduction to *Mrs. Dalloway*) plagued her all her life, was perhaps even more terrible. In the spring of 1941 Mrs. Woolf's hat and stick were found on the banks of a river near her home, where she had loved to walk; her body was recovered a few weeks later.

Drowning herself was, of course, a poetic as well as a physical act for Virginia Woolf: it expressed all of the longings to "merge" with things, to flow into and become part of the flux of the great sea of life, which were hinted at in *Mrs. Dalloway* and *The Waves*. But the anguish which drove the writer from literary contemplation of the act of suicide to the act itself was far more personal than poetic, as we can see from the note she felt her husband, Leonard Woolf: "I have the feeling that I shall go mad," she wrote. "I hear voices and cannot concentrate on my work. I have fought against it, but cannot fight any longer. I owe all my happiness in life to you. You have been so perfectly good. I cannot go and spoil your life." It is as though at a certain point in the lives of some artists - Keats, Lawrence, Beethoven, Van Gogh, Rilke, come to mind here too - the life and the art, which have, as it were, nourished each other from a distance, must fuse, must finally fuse and become one integrated expression of unique selfhood: as here, in the case of Virginia Woolf-metaphor becomes gesture, gesture, metaphor.

MRS. DALLOWAY

INTRODUCTION

YOKED BY VIOLENCE - THE METAPHYSICS OF THE DARK DOUBLE

JAMES JOYCE AND VIRGINIA WOOLF

Virginia Woolf viewed the conventional naturalistic novel of the nineteenth century as a bore, primarily because she thought that it reflected only the externals of life, giving a false or superficial view of life and character. Reality, Mrs. Woolf felt, was not a plotted narrative, but a composite of disparate personal experiences, the most significant of which are psychological. She found possibilities of ways to portray life, as she saw it, in the fiction of James Joyce. His method was also naturalistic, but in a new mode.

Virginia Woolf's *Mrs. Dalloway* is in many respects patterned after James Joyce's *Ulysses,* a book which was published three years earlier, in 1922, but which Mrs. Woolf had first seen in typescript, when Harriet Weaver asked her if she and her husband (they were then running the Hogarth Press) would publish it. Mrs. Woolf, who objected strongly to some aspects of *Ulysses*-she complained, for instance, of the indecency in the novel-must nevertheless have admired Joyce's technical prowess, for she later reported that she had finally read the book-despite moments of great boredom-with "spasms of wonder, of discovery." Joyce's depiction of the "stream of consciousness," for example, must have seemed to her to be exactly the sort of thing the modern novel should do. The job of the novelist, as she viewed it, is to convey subjective rather than objective reality, in the tradition of Joyce, James and Flaubert, rather than that of Zola, Balzac and George Moore.

STREAM OF CONSCIOUSNESS

The writers who first experimented with the stream-of-consciousness method, and who helped it to become a well-established aspect of twentieth-century fiction, were Dorothy Richardson, James Joyce, Virginia Woolf and William Faulkner. The technique which they innovated, however, is no longer considered "experimental"; it has been used by many writers since the 1930s.

Stream of consciousness is a **metaphor** coined by William James, philosopher-psychologist brother of the American novelist Henry James. The phrase, in the literary sense, indicates a particular approach to the presentation of psychological aspects of character in fiction. The concept behind the term, as William James used it, is that ideas and consciousness in general are fluid and shifting, rather than fixed. Consciousness, James stated, is a "teeming multiplicity of objects and relations" which are not logically ordered; they form a fluid flux ("a river or stream") of sensations, perceptions and conscious thoughts.

As a literary term, stream of consciousness refers to the presentation of a character's thoughts, emotional reactions, mental associations and images, etc., on an approximated preverbal level, with little or no direct comment or explanation by the author. This technique attempts to evoke directly the private psychic life and to depict subjective, as well as objective, reality. Virginia Woolf, for example, believed that an artist should express his private vision of reality through the description of the private psychic activity of individual characters.

Stream of consciousness represents mental activity that is on the borderline of conscious thought; it is depicted with the devices of association, word - and symbol-motifs, mental incoherence, and the reduction (or sometimes total disappearance) of grammatical **syntax** and punctuation to simulate the free flow of the character's mental life.

The stream-of-consciousness method makes use of four basic techniques: direct and indirect interior monologue, omniscient description and soliloquy. "Interior monologue" is a narrative technique (which the nineteenth-century writer Edouard Dujardin claimed to have used first) which is sometimes incorrectly used synonymously with stream of consciousness. It refers, however, to the presentation of thoughts more consciously controlled and on a level closer to the grammatical **syntax** of normal speech.

Direct interior monologues are those which are represented by negligible interference by the author. That is, consciousness is presented directly to the reader. The author is not present, the character is not speaking to anyone in the story, nor is he speaking to the reader. One of the most famous examples of this type of monologue is Molly's monologue at the close of James Joyce's *Ulysses*. The indirect interior monologue gives the reader a direct sense of the author's control over his material, because it uses third or second person, rather than first, and makes use of descriptive and expository methods (description and commentary) to present the monologue. There is also greater coherence and unity. Among the stream-of-consciousness writers mentioned above, Virginia Woolf relies most on indirect interior monologue.

The conventional device of omniscient description in a stream-of-consciousness novel refers to the technique of presenting the psychic content and processes of a character's mind in such a way that the omniscient author describes that person's consciousness through conventional narrative methods and description. This technique may be used alone or in combination with the other techniques. Dorothy Richardson used this approach rather consistently in the twelve volumes of *Pilgrimage* (1915-1935). She was the first novelist to deliberately employ a stream-of-consciousness technique.

The soliloquy differs from the interior monologue because it assumes an immediate audience. It therefore has much greater coherence, since its purpose is to communicate emotions and ideas which are related to a plot and action. The interior monologue, on the other hand, is used to communicate psychic identity. William Faulkner's *As I Lay Dying* makes use of the soliloquy for fifteen different characters. Virginia Woolf makes use of it in *The Waves*.

Such a concentration on the subjective, especially the idiosyncratic images of the individual mind, must necessarily involve a more than usual lyrical use of words, and the poetic possibilities of the Joycean novel also fascinated Mrs. Woolf. In an age in which, so it seemed to her, poetry no longer satisfied the literary hungers of the average reader, "the poetic novel," as

Leon Edel has noted, "represented a compromise." Prose fiction, Mrs. Woolf wrote, must take on "something of the exaltation of poetry" though retaining "much of the ordinariness of prose" - exactly, in fact, Joyce's attempt in works like *Ulysses* and *Finnegans Wake*.

All stream-of-consciousness fiction depends on the use of free association. The main differences between various techniques lie in the complexity and privacy of the free associations and the frequency with which they are used. For example, if the associations that an individual character makes are extremely private, if the private symbolism is very subjective and confidential, a stream-of-consciousness novel may be incoherent and difficult to interpret. This is true because the mental activity described is usually filled only with clues and suggestions which the reader has to unravel to understand their meaning. The more private the mental impressions and associations, the more private and evanescent the novel.

Other devices of stream-of-consciousness fiction include what critics call "cinematic" techniques. These include methods of handling time and space relationships that are similar to montage. (Mrs. Woolf makes considerable use of these devices in *Mrs. Dalloway*, as we shall see later.) "Montage" in the film sense refers to the use of a rapid succession of images or the overlapping of images to show the association of ideas. Translated into literary terms, this technique uses associations and images to allow for shifting back and forth in space and to intermingle past, present and future time. For example, a character may remain fixed in space while his consciousness moves across time; this technique results in what has been called a time-montage in which images or ideas from one time are super-imposed on another time. On the other hand, time may remain fixed while the spatial element changes - what is called the space-montage.

The space-montage does not always involve the presentation of the contents of a specific consciousness. Both of these methods are used to express movement or coexistence - the inner life simultaneously with the outer life and time simultaneously with space.

SIMULTANEITY

Virginia Woolf was particularly fascinated by Joyce's depiction of what we may call simultaneity - the interaction of events in time and space, such as, for example, the famous tenth ("Wandering Rocks") **episode** of *Ulysses* in which the viceregal cavalcade winds its way through Dublin, passing - and joining in its passage - all the major and most of the minor characters in the book. Indeed, she modeled the opening section of *Mrs. Dalloway* - and much of the structure of the book as a whole - on this technique of Joyce's. For just as the individual scenes in section ten of *Ulysses* are linked and unified by the progress of the viceregal cavalcade, so the entire book is organized around the separate but simultaneous progresses of Bloom and Dedalus through their city and through their day. And *Mrs. Dalloway* is similarly organized around the apparently disconnected but profoundly related journeys of Clarissa Dalloway and Septimus Warren Smith through a crucial day-again as in *Ulysses*, a day in June. Indeed, the relationship between the two central characters in *Mrs. Dalloway* is even more tenuous and - we might even say - **metaphysical** than the central relationship in *Ulysses*.

Bloom and Stephen do, after all, know each other long before they become Blephen and Stoom, and that mystically significant meeting in section seventeen is a meeting in the flesh as well as in the spirit. Plot as well as **theme**, drama as well as poetry demands it. But in *Mrs. Dalloway* the only connection between

Clarissa and Septimus is, as we have said, a metaphysical, or even metaphorical, one. Clarissa, hearing of Septimus' suicide, puts herself in his place; she recognizes that this unknown young man represents the shadowy underside of her life; he is her insane self, her doppelganger, her dark double.

CONCEPT OF THE DOPPELGANGER

A doppelganger (or doubleganger) is, as defined by *Webster's New World Dictionary,* "The ghost or wraith of a living person," but in literature, where the doppelganger has been a popular device since the early nineteenth century (cf. particularly the work of early nineteenth-century German writers like E.T.A. Hoffmann and Heinrich von Kleist), it has come gradually to take on a more profound meaning-to represent not simply the double or twin, the mirror image, of a character's personality, but often a kind of reversal of it, a negative image, a self which expresses all the dark and normally inexpressible (in Freudian terms "repressed") desires of the ordinary daytime self. A creation like Stevenson's Dr. Jekyll-Mr. Hyde is a good, and well-known, example of this: Dr. Jekyll, the enlightened scientist, is the conscious, socially acceptable self-as it were, the ego. Mr. Hyde, the brutish killer, is the dark underself, the inadmissible double - the id. Conrad's "The Secret Sharer" is another obvious example: Leggatt, the midnight visitor, not only represents the captain's own repressed impulses, but also what the captain himself might have become, under other circumstances-a kind of expression of the captain in another dimension or time-warp. A number of other nineteenth-century works employ the doubling mechanism (for the nineteenth century, with its pioneering studies of the mind-of schizophrenia, of the unconscious-was vitally interested in this concept). Mary Shelley's *Frankenstein,* for example, may be said to use it in a rather subtle way, for the

Hyde-like monster Frankenstein creates is in a sense the double of Frankenstein, the expression of a submerged and crippled part of his mind. Oscar Wilde's *The Picture of Dorian Gray*, too, is a variation on the doubling **theme**: Dorian, of course, has no really good self, but the secret of his picture is the secret of a kind of physical double, one who seems to take on himself - as Hyde does - the burden of evil, while the other, Dorian himself, seems to remain unscathed.

THE SANE AND THE INSANE

But if Hyde, Frankenstein's monster, and Dorian Gray's picture all must bear the burden of evil, Septimus Warren Smith, Mrs. Dalloway's double in Virginia Woolf's novel, must bear instead, as Virginia Woolf declared, the burden of insanity and, as we shall see, of a preternaturally heightened consciousness, a consciousness especially of the world's wrongs, which Clarissa Dalloway herself does not seem to have. Perhaps this vision of the world "as seen by the sane and the insane side by side" was an outgrowth of Mrs. Woolf's own recurrent bouts of mental illness. She was apparently prey to fits of anxiety, depression, and other symptoms on and off throughout her life, but especially just after she had finished a novel. In the end, indeed, she committed suicide to avoid succumbing to another attack and becoming a burden to her husband as well as herself. But whatever his genesis, Septimus, Clarissa's dark double, solved a technical as well as a psychological problem for Mrs. Woolf. She had originally planned to have Clarissa commit suicide at the end of the book, an act which would demonstrate the hollowness of her society-matron life, her life as a "perfect hostess." Instead, however, she chose a subtler and more **metaphysical** way of illuminating Clarissa's life; she interwove Clarissa's seemingly "normal" thoughts and feelings with the supposedly "abnormal" consciousness of Septimus and in the end, through Septimus' suicide and Clarissa's intense reaction to it, she made her final point about Clarissa. Whether this technique was entirely successful has been debated by a number of critics, and though most concede the brilliance of Mrs. Woolf's style and the wit (in the sense of intelligence rather than humor) of her plan, a majority remain, finally, unmoved by *Mrs. Dalloway.* The connection between Clarissa Dalloway and Septimus Warren Smith is perhaps, at last, too tenuous, too **metaphysical**; like terms of a Cowley **metaphor**, they are yoked by violence, not necessity, and a reader's response to their juxtaposition is cerebral rather than emotional.

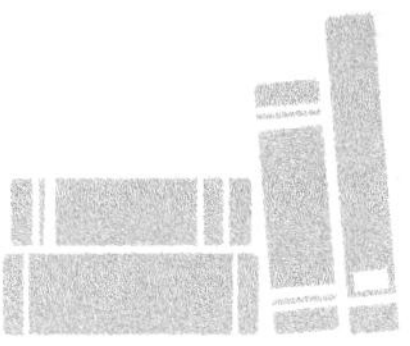

MRS. DALLOWAY

A CRITICAL ANALYSIS

UNIFIED DESIGN

Mrs. Dalloway is unified in much the same way as Joyce's *Ulysses.* It takes place within twenty-four hours in the month of June, it takes place in the city of London (one district), and it involves two major characters. (*Ulysses* takes place in one day in June in Dublin and is centered around the adventures of Bloom and Dedalus.) And yet the time involved is eighteen years and events occur from India to England. Therefore, the outer unities, as it were, are superimposed on a narrative which lacks them. A fairly static focal point is provided for the reader's mind to return to while he is following the convoluted associations in the various characters' consciousnesses.

THE OPENING

In the extraordinary opening pages of *Mrs. Dalloway,* Virginia Woolf introduces fragile, ladylike Clarissa Dalloway by means of an extended indirect interior monologue. Though we experience briefly the thoughts of many among a large group of characters, it is Clarissa Dalloway's mind that is all - pervasive. It is her consciousness through which the sights and sounds of London are exquisitely filtered. From the first we are introduced to her way of looking at things, her preoccupation with society, her fears and fancies and-most important of all-her memories. Much of the significant action of the novel takes place in the past, in Clarissa's memory (and later in Peter Walsh's).

Unlike many of the interior monologues in Joyce's *Ulysses*, Mrs. Woolf's novel is comparatively coherent. Compared to Joyce, it is much more conventional. The author is present throughout (in such expressions as "she thought") and the narrative is in the third person. *Mrs. Dalloway* has a deliberate incoherence, however, a trait distinctly "modern" in the history of the novel. References and meanings are intentionally vague and not explained. The narrative also has a strong element of disunity, as Mrs. Dalloway's mind wanders from one subject to another.

Mrs. Woolf often makes use of cinematic devices in the opening pages of the novel. The spatial element is stationary; we stay with Clarissa's consciousness for the most part. The images present in this time-montage are quite numerous, however, both in diversity of subject matter and in time of happening (time shifts quickly from the far past to the present to the future). The thing which unifies a passage of this sort is a character's consciousness-i.e., Clarissa's mind.

Virginia Woolf makes superb use of the space-montage in the scene in which the airplane is skywriting. Time remains static, but we are given a cross-section view of London as various people in the city respond to the same event. We are introduced to Septimus Warren Smith, who is to be-in the symbolic terms of the novel - the heroine's double. They never meet, but they are joined in time in this passage, and we are introduced to both of their psyches in this scene. The plane is the unifying device, as well as the central focus in the montage.

OTHER PERSPECTIVES

Throughout the novel, other characters occasionally provide us with a perspective on the heroine which her own thoughts could not supply. Here is one of the advantages of the author's use of the Joycean technique of simultaneity; where a more traditional writer-fearful of flitting from mind to mind-would have had to let his heroine look in a mirror and think about what she saw in the glass, Virginia Woolf simply switches quickly to another consciousness, another point of view. This second point of view is one which at the same time the heroine is thinking one set of thoughts, thinks wholly different thoughts about her, thus giving her, as it were, another dimension of reality.

IMAGERY AND SYMBOLISM

An image is a word or group of words used to suggest a visual picture or other sensory experience. Images are figurative comparisons, usually in the form of **metaphors** or similes. The poetic quality of both *Mrs. Dalloway* and *To the Lighthouse* owes its potency to an impressionistic use of imagery. Impressionism in painting denotes a style which attempts to convey an impression of something rather than a naturalistic representation or a stylized, romantic representation. Impressionism in literature, particularly in lyrical poetry, is an attempt to convey subjective, personal impressions of individual experiences. Mrs. Woolf's impressionistic **imagery** is highly subjective-it expresses one of her character's private emotional estimates of what is perceived, or the author describes a scene in highly figurative terms-relying on the **connotations** of words to evoke a mood or give an impression of a scene, rather than a literal picture. (See the discussion of Mrs. Woolf's poetic techniques in the later discussion of *To the Lighthouse.*)

In addition, stream-of-consciousness writers, particularly Virginia Woolf, rely on the use of symbolism to suggest several levels of meaning. It is once again often a very private symbolism (that is, the symbol has a different personal significance to each character) to suggest the privacy of the individual mind, as well as to stand for ideas that are peculiar to one particular character. (Mrs. Woolf was undoubtedly influenced by a number of modern philosophers who suggest that symbol-formation is a primary mental process which is prior to association or ideation.)

Big Ben is a sound image of both structural and symbolic importance in *Mrs. Dalloway.* Throughout the day it counts out the hours, marking the progress of all the characters-Clarissa, Peter, Richard, Septimus and Lucrezia-toward evening and the **climax** of their interwoven journeys. (Mrs. Woolf's use of the symbolic Lighthouse in *To the Lighthouse* will reveal the manner in which she uses a symbolic structure to give coherence to the stream of consciousness which pervades the novel.)

The symbolic significance of the motorcar is never precisely pinpointed, but it represents, on one level at least, the majesty of England, the power and mystery of the "Establishment." On another level, the motorcar, with its enigmatic, unidentified passenger, may represent death. It is interesting to note, in this connection, that the appearance of the car is closely associated with the first entrance of the character we have called Mrs. Dalloway's dark double, the mad (shell-shocked) poet, Septimus Warren Smith. The motorcar, like the airplane, is used as a spatial device to unify the reactions of Clarissa, Septimus Lucrezia and others.

The motorcar unites a variety of social classes as they respond to it with curiosity, terror or patriotism. Like the scene of the viceregal cavalcade in *Ulysses,* this kaleidoscopic scene in *Mrs. Dalloway* is meant also to convey the complexity of the city and the variety - the multiplicity - of its life.

A particularly impressive passage suggests the dual identity of the passenger in the car. For the face that will be known when London is covered over with grass is not only the coined face of the Queen, but the skull, the death's head of power. And the subtle association set up here of England's majesty, of established power and authority, with death, is one that persists throughout the novel.

Later in the story, there is another motorcar of symbolic significance, outside Sir William Bradshaw's office. Like the earlier motorcar, it is also a symbol of the power and coldness that separate Septimus and Lucrezia from Sir William and his smug, self-confident world.

THE ESTABLISHMENT

Clarissa's thoughts sketch a perfectly idealized picture of established, upper-class, early twentieth-century London, a society which Mrs. Woolf implies has little right to exist, except in the minds of matrons like Clarissa. Virginia Woolf, herself a part of the British Establishment, was not exactly a fiery revolutionary, however, almost in spite of herself, in spite of whatever social theories she had, she could not help singing the praises of this way of life, but we are meant also to see its hollowness, superficiality and coldness-in Clarissa herself. All of the members of Clarissa's social class are part of an empire, an order, a way of life, which is-even as it blithely goes about its summery business-doomed, dying, almost dead. The symbol of the motorcar, as we suggested above, conveys this idea.

Much more than Clarissa, however, the portly, pompous, sanctimonious Hugh Whitbread embodies the faults of self-righteous, imperial England and of the social-climbing bourgeoisie with their mindless respect for anything aristocratic. Hugh, with his gift for platitudinous phrases, his impeccable tailoring, and his reverence for royalty, not only represents the upper-class Establishment, but also raises the question of its fitness to govern in a modern, postwar world.

Because Hugh is in a sense responsible for the plight of the lower classes, he is similar to the self-righteous Henry Wilcox of *Howards End* (a novel written by Mrs. Woolf's Bloomsbury colleague, E. M. Forster), just as Doris Kilman is comparable to the oppressed Leonard Bast of that book. For Henry Wilcox, we actually see in *Howards End*, has corrupted and discarded the woman who is later to become Leonard's wife. Mr. Wilcox is literally responsible for her fate, just as Hugh is, when Sally, in *Mrs. Dalloway,* accuses him of being figuratively responsible for the plight of prostitutes.

If Hugh represents all that is wrong with the Establishment-its mindlessness, its stuffiness, its superficial values-Richard Dalloway represents what is right with it: the fact that basically it means well. Though Richard is also a member of the upper class, he represents a kind of stock Englishman-goodhearted, sensible, kind, but unimaginative. In Virginia Woolf's view, the British government (the majesty of England) does mean well, despite its materialistic values, the corruption of business, the poverty of people like Doris Kilman and the prostitutes in Piccadilly, and the madness of Septimus induced by war. A hardworking colonial administrator like Peter Walsh-sprung from a long line of such men-really does want to do right by India. Lady Burton really does hope to help the poor. Dr. Holmes (though not Sir William Bradshaw) is, while hopelessly stupid, really anxious to help Septimus. This, for Virginia Woolf, is England's absolution: her good intentions for the most part make her sins venial, not mortal.

(And in *Howards End,* too, Forster has the Schlegel sisters recognize that Henry Wilcox-for all his complacency and self-righteousness-is one of those who makes the world's wheels, the wheels of progress, go around. The Bloomsbury philosophy which Virginia Woolf and Forster shared is, finally, moderate; without condoning the evils of the Establishment, without ignoring its hollowness of heart, Bloomsbury grants that the Establishment often means well and often gets things done that the individual could never do.)

This virtue of the Establishment-as represented in Richard-is to some extent an explanation for Clarissa's rigid adherence to **convention**. Clarissa is a realist, a woman who is only too well aware of her own coldness and of the faults of her way of life and of her class. Early in the novel, when Clarissa reminisces about Peter Walsh, the reader gets a very clear idea of the nature of Clarissa's value and of her essential lack of emotional warmth. Her values often parallel those of Hugh Whitbread and her kind: worldly success-rank, reputation, riches - these are everything, or almost everything, to Clarissa. Knowing what she is, Clarissa, the reader guesses, would not deceive herself about the future of this life. Since she can see no other way of life possible, she will probably endure the guilt it necessitates in order to partake in its pleasures.

By far the most personally repugnant, as well as the most truly evil representative of the Establishment, in Virginia Woolf's eyes, is Sir William Bradshaw. In her description of him, Mrs. Woolf allows her **irony** to become savage. Sir William, a nouveau-riche, delights in the power and wealth that his high standing in his profession gives him. Utterly without the capacity for love or compassion, he enjoys manipulating lives for his own sake, according to this own narrowly righteous - and often hypocritical - standards.

Elizabeth Dalloway one might call the product of the Establishment. She is amenable, vapid and rather vacuous - just what one would expect a dutiful but unawakened debutante to be. She has been pampered and her thoughts do not stray beyond the London social bustle and comfortable country life. She combines her father's calm competence with her mother's love of the pure rush and flux and variety of life.

SNOBBERY

Needless to say, Clarissa is a snob. The passages which describe her relationship to Doris Kilman demonstrate this. Clarissa's hatred for Doris (and this hatred is probably the most intense emotion she feels in the course of the book) is rooted in guilt, that most universal motive for hostility.

It is the specter of the lower classes that Miss Kilman represents - the world of servants and slums which supports and makes possible the airy grace of Clarissa Dalloway's parties. Like Leonard Bast, the downtrodden clerk in Forster's *Howards End,* she reminds the wealthy and the privileged of the grimy underside of their lives, of the ugliness they can afford to disregard, and of the responsibility their

Establishment, their rule, must take for poverty, war and discontent.

Of course, as in *Howards End,* having understood the predicament of Doris Kilman, we do not automatically side with her and against Clarissa Dalloway, her "oppressor." Moral matters are not so black and white in either Woolf or Forster. Like Leonard Bast, Doris Kilman is in many respects an unpleasant, unsympathetic character, self-pitying and unattractive. And unlike Leonard, who sometimes, almost despite himself, displays a kind of pathetic, forlorn charm, Doris Kilman is righteously, grotesquely religious-indeed, evangelical. And we can at least understand why this grimy evangelism-to which she seems in part to have converted Elizabeth Dalloway-would set Clarissa against her. For despite her many self-deceptions, Clarissa is at bottom a spiritual realist, one who dare not delude herself, despite her flirtations with the notion of a kind of social immortality, about life's dangers and death's attractions.

Despite the many facets and implications of the relationship between Doris and Clarissa, however, and despite its dramatic and thematic centrality, it is one of the least successful parts of the book. It was one of Virginia Woolf's failings (as, indeed, it was to a lesser extent one of Forster's) that she could not empathize with the "lower classes" because of the snobbery implicit in her own Establishment background. Though we are told a good deal about Doris, we never feel or believe in her hostility, grubbiness and unpleasantness for ourselves, or at least not at the same as we believe (as Virginia Woolf evidently wants us to) in the depth of her attachment for Elizabeth and the reality of Elizabeth's response to her. With her lower-class evangelism and bitter resentment of Clarissa, she is a cardboard character, clearly created to fill an obvious need in the novel for a wider spectrum of social and emotional representation. Nevertheless, there is one essential respect in which Doris as a character functions successfully in the novel-as a demonstration of the failure of Clarissa's relationship with her daughter. This failure represents, as well, her other emotional failures - the hollowness behind her facade of perfect hostess, and the frigidity behind her mask of perfect wife.

MIDDLE AGE AND DEATH

Clarissa's thoughts express not only her idea of herself, but also Virginia Woolf's interest in writing a book about middle age, the stage of life when - the personality, the fate, being fixed - the past begins to play an increasingly large part in the present, and there is "no more marrying, no more having children," but only meditation on what was done and what not done, what was achieved and what not achieved. Thus, Clarissa's mind is full of memories of Peter Walsh, Doris Kilman and others.

Clarissa, though she has long since lost all the intellectual and artistic interests of her youth, has a sense of the danger and difficulty of life; death, which she is continually trying to define for herself, both terrifies and attracts her. She meditates on a snatch of verse from Shakespeare, the dirge-lyric from *Cymbeline*: "Fear no more the heat o' the sun/ Nor the furious winter rages." The seductive silence of death, of impervious peace, beckons her as-later, more powerfully- it beckons Septimus Warren Smith, Clarissa's dark double. Perhaps because of both her illness and her age, however, life, so Clarissa thinks, is what she really loves; it is her real passion. But when she broods about death it seems to her to represent the end of desire and fear. The lines from *Cymbeline* suggest that death is a welcome release from the burden of life.

At the same time, however, Clarissa is life-oriented enough to be slightly jealous of Peter's zest and involvement in life and love. Her rationalizations for why she is glad she didn't marry him are hardly convincing to the reader. They seem tinged with pain and regret.

Unlike Clarissa (perhaps because he is an idealist and she is a realist), Peter refuses to accept or even face the fact of his age. His affair with Daisy is a sign of his rebellion against age and against propriety. But he has always been a rebel. When young he was in rebellion against the established order of society. Now, grown, middle-aged, he is a Don Quixote, tilting against the windmill of time.

The **themes** of middle age and death are also suggested in Peter's encounter with the nurse. The set-piece that follows is a brilliant example of Virginia Woolf's lyrical skill. Peter-symbol for the middle-aged traveler, lonely and time-weary-encounters a kind of earth-mother who offers charity and absolution. This figure suggests not only nature, the world-spirit, but also death, for is not nature death as well as life?

When Septimus mistakes Peter for Evans, there is a further suggestion of death, as well as a comment of Peter's personality. The suggestion here is the death of the Establishment of which Peter, despite himself, is a part.

Mrs. Dalloway is, as we have seen, drenched in thoughts of death. Both Clarissa and Septimus - and Peter Walsh, too - long with at least a part of themselves for the perfection of peace and stillness which is death. And so here death is the nurse who offers understanding.

THE WAR

Imagery of death surrounds Septimus; there is always a sharp contrast between the horror of Septimus' thoughts and the bright June day. As he broods over the death of his friend, the reader became aware that war is the true villain of the novel, the cause of despair, horror and death, the turning point for individual lives as well as for society as a whole. Since the war, both man and society, Mrs. Woolf seems to be trying to show, have been sick; they are dying or drenched in death: there is no going back, Virginia Woolf sees, to what now seems the Edenlike innocence of the pre-war world-Mrs. Dalloway's girlhood at Bourton, Septimus Warren Smith's young dream of Shakespeare.

This use of the War, World War I, as a turning point, a kind of fall from grace, is not unique in *Mrs. Dalloway.* Throughout many of her later novels, Virginia Woolf (who, like most British intellectuals, felt keenly the horror and tragedy of this first "worldwide" conflagration, this brutal "war to end war") was preoccupied with the disastrous effect of the War on European society. Of course, too, she was not alone in this preoccupation: writers like Thomas Mann (on the continent) and D.H. Lawrence (in England) were also preoccupied with the cataclysmic effects of the War and to them, too, it signified Europe's fall from grace and the emergence of a tortured modern consciousness, a deranged and death-seeking mind like, apparently, the mind of Septimus Warren Smith. Yet, paradoxically enough, though Septimus' consciousness seems mad, we shall see by the end of the novel that, with his vulnerability, his acute sensitivity to hypocrisy, his Blakelike pronouncements against killing and in favor of love, Septimus is, in a sense, the sanest and certainly the most aware most truthful character in the novel. The righteously blind Sir William with his evil need for power over others, the smugly self-confident Holmes and hollow-hearted

Hugh Whitbread - these are the real madmen, dead souls and dealers in the death of the soul.

Peter's attitude toward war is in sharp contrast to Septimus'. Peter respects the training and ideals of patriotic fidelity and duty of young recruits. Septimus, whose experience of war is real, well-founded, free of patriotic sentimentality, comes closer to expressing Virginia Woolf's own views-with his dark, mad apprehensions of society. Despite his tirades against sentimentality, despite his liberated thoughts, Peter suffers from a certain intellectual shabbiness; he has gone a bit threadbare, mentally; the edges of his thoughts fray and ravel.

EMOTIONAL STERILITY

There are numerous references to indicate that Clarissa is a prude with an unusually cold, arrogant, unimaginative personality. She meditates on her own central coldness - a coldness which has caused her, ultimately, to fail in the emotional as well as - presumably - the sexual relationship of marriage. Her memories of Peter Walsh also suggest this same problem. For example, Clarissa seems most obviously to lack motherliness. The person in her orbit whom she apparently has affected least in her own daughter, Elizabeth, who has fallen, instead, under the spell of the clumsy and hostile Doris Kilman.

Clarissa's warmth seems to have been reserved for Sally Seton. Her passion for Sally was apparently one of the few really intense emotions Clarissa ever felt in her life, and this fact is significant for two reasons. First, Sally seems to have represented to Clarissa an intellectual flowering which has long since withered. There was a time when she was as capable of questioning established authority as Septimus or even Peter himself. Now, however, her reading is confined to memoirs and her greatest ambition apparently is to entertain the Prime Minister, the symbol-as Mrs. Woolf sees him-of England's dying majesty. However, when the reader meets Sally, she is rather ordinary and dull and lacks her youthful fire and idealism, although middle age has not robbed her of her impetuous warmheartedness.

Secondly, Clarissa's crush on Sally is significant because it reveals, interestingly enough, that only with a woman could the virginal Mrs. Dalloway ever feel emotional warmth-always and only with women, where no sexual and in a certain sense no emotional fulfillment is possible. Thus the tendency to be "charmed" by women is still part of her central coldness, her inability to yield herself on her independence to a larger relationship. Clarissa's withdrawal is the "death of her soul," the death of warmth and love. Emotional sterility is not Clarissa's problem alone. Doris Kilman-a hostile, self-pitying, bitter, possessive, jealous, and outraged feminist-is also a sterile person. She is capable of a passionate attachment to Elizabeth Dalloway and to religion, it is true, but both attachments seem neurotically motivated by hatred, instead of by love. By comparison, Clarissa seems much warmer. She at least has the ability to relate to people and to allow them to be themselves. Intrusive, jealous Doris, with her desire to dominate, her "pious" urge to power is, in Mrs. Woolf's view, a villain of the same order (though not to the same degree) as Sir William Bradshaw - though perhaps, unlike Sir William, a victim too. But villain and victim, what righteous Doris Kilman wants is what smug Sir William wants: to impose one's will, to own, to manipulate.

The enigma of others fascinates Clarissa, the enigma of other people who are not oneself and yet who exist in their strangeness, variety and self-sufficiency like plants which one need not pluck or identify or alter (as Doris or Sir William would) to fully apprehend.

SUPERFICIAL VALUES

Clarissa's emotional sterility is intimately tied to her superficial values. She is ambitious for success in the world's eyes. Her marriage to Richard rather than Peter is a sign of that ambition. Her conventionality, her mindless respect for the authority of society, is symptomatic of the death of individual judgment and love. Her soul is sterile. She has lost the faculty which judges and loves and commits itself emotionally without respect to the views of established authority. Her values do not reflect a concern for important, profound issues and aspects of life; Clarissa's mind is preoccupied with the London social season. Like Hugh, she is guilty of the complacency of a social class that is sealed off in its careful, elegant world of peers and parties. Theirs is a world as orderly and artificial as a single, well-run, many-servanted household that perpetuates, indeed often exploits, poverty to its own ends.

Clarissa's main interest is in being a social success, and she has achieved this through her parties, her raison d'etre. Clarissa loves parties because deep down, for all her faults, she loves life, its variety and its vitality. Like Mrs. Dalloway herself, we come to see that Virginia Woolf feels that Clarissa's great gift is the gift for life, and that her parties are the outgrowth of this talent. Like Mrs. Ramsay in *To the Lighthouse,* Clarissa Dalloway has the gift of ordering her environment, organizing isolated individuals into a coherent social whole, simply by being herself and gaining their love or affection. But as we have seen here already, and as we shall see in *To the Lighthouse,* where Clarissa Dalloway often fails to fully and compassionately use her gift, where she is often frivolous, superficial and cold, Mrs. Ramsay is the very embodiment of charity and she uses her gift for structuring the life around her accordingly. Just as Mrs. Ramsay's family dinner and her great pot of boeuf en daube were her works of art, her way of shaping the universe in her own image, so Clarissa's dazzling evening, her party, is her work of art. But her coldness, of course, is still there at the center; and the party ends as a hollow triumph, a triumph which is unsatisfying.

SEPTIMUS

Septimus, Clarissa's dark double and her opposite, is intelligent, idealistic, and sensitive, a man with the soul of a poet who has not been able to withstand the ravages of life and war. His self-education and literary dreams were swallowed up in the lonely life of the city; they were eventually destroyed by war, which left him in a state of hopelessly unstable neurosis. (To continue the Forster analogy, this description of Septimus sounds much like the description of Leonard Bast, the half-educated clerk in *Howards End*. Septimus is clearly superior to Leonard in both talent and education, but the two have in common the all-important fact that through no fault of their own, but through the rigid class structure of English society, they are shut out from all civilization-all the elegance and ease which might be much more meaningful to them than it is to the thick-skinned Hugh Whitbread and Henry Wilcox of England.)

Septimus' war experiences destroyed him emotionally. Confronted with the horror of his own indifference to values, and his emotional isolation from people and things, he crosses over the threshold of mental illness. While Clarissa has been able to accept and live with that central coldness in herself, Septimus her dark double, the mad self who acts out (in the terms of the novel) her most terrible fantasies-cannot accept a life without feeling. His solution is to recoil from the world in horror at the hypocrisy and corruption he sees around him. His withdrawal causes Lucrezia as much pain as he himself experiences. (It is interesting to note that just as Septimus struggles to feel love and hate, to bring his soul to life with emotion, Doris Kelman seeks to destroy feeling in herself.) Rezia, the spirit of love and laughter, is Septimus' only hope for a cure, but she cannot hope to compete with the powers of destruction. Septimus' final act is an act of queer courage, of defiance, against the righteous obtuseness that he felt he could escape only in death. In the end, the powers of destruction-Dr. Holmes and his sort-triumph.

When the relationship between Clarissa and Septimus dramatically coalesces, Clarissa, in a moment of insight, is somehow more reconciled to the idea of death than she has ever been before. She feels a mysterious kinship with Septimus and is able to understand that Septimus' final act was his way of both defying the world and at the same time trying to communicate with it. Septimus has defied death: in one sense, the power of the physical fear of death, and in another sense, the spiritual death with which Sir William Bradshaw threatened him.

The old woman who fascinates Clarissa at different times in the novel also influences her thoughts about Septimus and death. This old woman seems to represent death, to which one must become reconciled in the middle of life, for death comes as naturally as the old woman's sleep in the midst of the long party of life.

MR. AND MRS. DALLOWAY

The relationship between Richard and Clarissa is devoid of warmth. Richard is sentimental, naive and well-intentioned. He is anxious to express his love to Clarissa, but he fails because he combines earnestness with the shyness and awkwardness of a young man. Complete communication-putting all their feelings into words-is impossible for both of them. Impossible for Richard because he is somewhat obtuse, impossible for Clarissa because of her coldness and her pervasive **realism**. There is a gulf between them which Clarissa, at least, is not interested in crossing. Interestingly enough, Clarissa's spiritual virginity has its advantages: it gives her that reticence, that respect for the privacy of others, which makes her a disciplined personality as well as a social success.

TRIUMPHANT FEMININITY

We may say that Clarissa's quality of enduring vitality, of triumphant femininity, is the trait which most fascinated Virginia Woolf in both Clarissa and Mrs. Ramsay and which impelled her to write the books she did about both women. The strong, enduring, enigmatic female character was a type which held special fascination for her, perhaps because her own mother was apparently such a woman and perhaps, too, because the type is one which has immemorially interested writers. And it was, after all, of particular interest to many writers in Mrs. Woolf's era, as witness James Joyce's portrait of Molly Bloom in *Ulysses* and E. M. Forster's use of the first Mrs. Wilcox in *Howards End* or of Mrs. Moore in *A Passage to India.*

Clarissa's significance, as we noted earlier, like Mrs. Ramsay's is the ability to generate excitement, and her enigmatic mixture of qualities-in Clarissa's case, virginity, sensitivity, ambition, realism-which makes her in her small circle the hub of the wheel, the focal point around which all else spins, past and present melting into a single shimmering blur in the great whirl and waltz of life about her, the still center.

SUBJECTIVITY

In *Mrs. Dalloway* there is little plot to speak of. Mrs. Woolf's focus, as we indicated in the introduction, is upon the world as it is reflected through the minds of characters who form the background of the novel - their extremely subjective impressions of one another and of the events in which they take part. This subjectivity results in a rising and falling flux of mental impressions, images, thoughts and emotions, which bring the characters into alternately dim and sharp focus as we get to know them.

The novel is built around small moments of perception or insight which the various characters experience. They are drawn together in space (by sharing similar experiences, sights and sounds) and in time (through memory and conscious analysis). The result is a picture of many different lives lived simultaneously, lives which seem mystically interwoven in a loose mosaic of psychic, temporal and spatial experience. Even when characters do not know one another personally, they are drawn together across time or space, sometimes affecting one another with no awareness that they are doing so. Their experiences occur against a backdrop of the city of London which is all the more vivid for its strange, almost hallucinatory quality which results when the hustle and bustle of a city is subjectively reflected and refracted through the eyes of several characters simultaneously.

MRS. DALLOWAY

CHARACTER ANALYSES

CLARISSA DALLOWAY

On the surface, Clarissa Dalloway must seem like a conventional, rather frivolous, elegant society woman. But as we quickly learn, there is more to Clarissa than her elegance; she has talents which go beyond frivolity. First of all, as she herself recognizes, she has an extraordinary talent for knowing people, for sensing almost instinctively whether they are friends or enemies. Second, as a kind of inevitable concomitant of this social instinct, Clarissa is a perfect hostess. Ambitious, something of a "schemer," worldly, fashionable, she pours most of her creativity and social warmth into the parties which, for her, have become a way of ordering the world, of arranging reality into pleasing and enduring patterns (much as Mrs. Ramsay in *To the Lighthouse* orders reality through love). Finally, Clarissa has a certain absolute internal reserve, close to frigidity, which is perhaps the quality which makes her most enigmatic, most mysteriously fascinating. There is ample evidence of Clarissa's emotional sterility: her ambitious worldliness and her central coldness, both of which tend to cut her off from the love and the honest openness with people which should by rights come naturally to someone with a social instinct as strong as hers. The whole of *Mrs. Dalloway*, however, is after all an exploration of Clarissa's character in general and of "the death of her soul" in particular. Despite her central coldness, however, the novel becomes, finally, a justification for her character.

PETER WALSH

Peter is Clarissa's harshest critic, a rather over-romantic middle-aged man, a hard-working colonial (Indian) administrator, who has been a failure in the world's eyes. Throughout the novel, he is Clarissa's romantic interest, to one degree or another, and has the clearest understanding of her personality.

RICHARD DALLOWAY

An embodiment of all that is right with the English gentleman, Richard Dalloway is a reasonably successful politician. He is not exceptionally bright - not an intellectual like Peter Walsh - but neither is he smug, insolent and overbearing like Hugh Whitbread. Moreover, Richard is sincere, well-meaning, very much in love with his wife, and anxious to do whatever good he can in the world.

HUGH WHITBREAD

If Richard Dalloway represents what is right about the English gentleman, Hugh Whitbread represents everything that is wrong with the breed. Well-dressed (perfectly upholstered, really), wealthy, a social-climber, Hugh happily runs around with dispatch boxes and - in effect - polishes the shoes of royalty.

Worst of all, he is insufferably rude - insolent and boorish - to his "inferiors" - to clerks and servants who can't do him any good socially.

SEPTIMUS WARREN SMITH

Intended by Virginia Woolf to serve, symbolically, as Clarissa's "double," a kind of insane version of the presumably sane "perfect hostess" Mrs. Dalloway, Septimus Warren Smith is a lower-middle-class young man of literary proclivities. Neurotic and fanatic, Septimus' problem parallels Clarissa's: she is essentially a cold person and he cannot relate to people emotionally either.

LUCREZIA WARREN SMITH

Rezia is a gay, ebullient, charming and warm-hearted Italian girl. She represents the spirit of love and laughter in Septimus' life, but she fails to save him from self-destruction.

DR. HOLMES

A local general practitioner, Dr. Holmes is an unimaginative but well intentioned man who mouths foolish platitudes instead of offering real warmth.

SIR WILLIAM BRADSHAW

If there is a villain in *Mrs. Dalloway,* Sir William is that creature. An ambitious, self-centered psychiatrist-totally without warmth or love or interest in his fellow-men he cares only for the power that his profession gives him, power to manipulate the lives of others, power to intrude, to meddle, to interfere.

ELIZABETH DALLOWAY

Clarissa's teenage daughter is a shy, inarticulate girl. She has just "come out" in society but she has little interest in the social whirl, unlike her mother. Like her father she loves the country and country-life, and like him she would like to "help people." She has inherited some of her mother's fondness for the London bustle too, though, and it is plain that her personality is still in the process of being formed.

DORIS KILMAN

One of the most puzzling characters in the book is Doris Kilman, the only character who arouses real passion in Clarissa Dalloway. The passion she arouses, however, is a passion of hate, and we tend to be somewhat unnerved by it, since it seems that Miss Kilman should, if anything, be an object of pity. Unattractive, poor, lumpy, intense, Doris Kilman seems to exercise quite a power over Elizabeth Dalloway. Miss Kilman is passionately fond of Elizabeth; indeed, her only two passions are this one for Elizabeth and an evangelistic religious fervor which has helped her to adjust to the unpleasantness of her life. Clarissa Dalloway hates her, however, because of her relationship to Elizabeth and because she seems to be the embodiment of the will-to-power, the will to dominate and meddle in the lives of others.

SALLY SETON

Clarissa's girlhood friend, a beautiful and daring young woman, has grown into a rather ordinary middle-aged woman. She is married to a rich man, and lives a rather bourgeois though expensive life. Middle age has robbed her of her youthful fire and intellectual idealism.

LADY BRUTON

A politically inclined peeress, Lady Bruton has a rather masculine mind (or so she likes to think), and therefore, although she has known Clarissa for many years, the two do not get on particularly well together-for Clarissa is, after all, despite her coldness, a totally feminine creature.

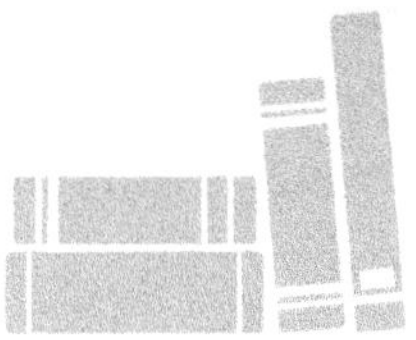

TO THE LIGHTHOUSE

OF TIME AND THE ARTIST: INTRODUCTION

TIME AND ART

If *The Waves* is the most experimental and "extreme" of Virginia Woolf's books, *Orlando* the most lighthearted and *Mrs. Dalloway* in a sense the most enigmatic, *To the Lighthouse* is for most readers the most moving and, as a result, may be considered really the most successful. Moreover, it makes the most interesting and perhaps the most poetic use of time. Where in *Mrs. Dalloway* the author expanded the events of a seventeen-hour period, one day in the life of a London society woman, into the material of a novel; where in *Orlando* she contracted four centuries into a single lifetime; in *To the Lighthouse* (as in *The Waves*) she distorts time in a more complicated way, both expanding and contracting it, for while the first section of the book deals, like *Mrs. Dalloway,* with the events of a single day, indeed of a single afternoon, the second section, a kind of poetic bridge passage, both expands and contracts time-expands a single night, the night following the afternoon of part one, into a period of ten years, and by doing so contracts the passage of ten years into a single night. Section three, finally, deals with the events of a single morning as though they followed naturally upon the afternoon ten years before.

Virginia Woolf was helped to this radical use of time, as many critics have pointed out, by her reading of two French thinkers who have, indeed, affected most contemporary thought on the subject. The first, Henri Bergson, undoubtedly influenced the second, Marcel Proust, but in any case, whatever their mutual interaction, between them they helped remold the traditional chronology of the novel. Time, as Bergson saw it, is simply a measure of the duration of the individual, of the accretion of the past; duration-la duree-is a function of "the invisible progress of the past, which gnaws into the future." And amid the flux and variety of experience, of the present which is so ungraspably, so continually receding into the past, one cannot help, as Proust saw too, perceiving the two-past and present-as, in a sense, simultaneous. For so evanescent is the present that even as we experience it, it is part of the past, and so immediate, then, is the past, that we often perceive it-at least its most significant moments-as if it were part of the present. Thus memory becomes central, not only in Bergson's philosophy, but in the novels of writers like Proust and Virginia Woolf. In *Mrs. Dalloway*, for instance, half the action takes place in memory, in the past, and in *To the Lighthouse* the present of section three can only finally be completed by Lily's return in thought to the past of section one.

Lily's centrality in section three is significant, for in all this, of course, the artist plays a major role. It is he, finally, and only he, after all, who fixes the flux, the tide of sensation and memory, in a more permanent framework: he explores and recreates the past in his novel or poem or play or picture. It is he who seizes the receding image-as Lily Briscoe seizes the fading and half-forgotten yet still somehow living image of Mrs. Ramsay - and fixes it perpetually in art.

THE USES OF AUTOBIOGRAPHY

But the moving power of *To the Lighthouse* is not, finally, a result of its experimental distortion of time: *Mrs. Dalloway, Orlando* and *The Waves,* though not so profoundly poignant, all do, after all, make similar experiments. The power of *To the Lighthouse* probably inheres, rather, in the exceedingly personal importance of its subject-matter to Virginia Woolf. For while the subjects of *Mrs. Dalloway, Orlando, The Waves* - and (obviously) all of her novels - must have had some keen significance to Mrs. Woolf as an artist (otherwise she would not have bothered to write them, after all), *To the Lighthouse,* more than any of the others, had intense meaning to her as a person. The family pictured, as so many critics and biographers have noted, is quite plainly her own: Mrs. Ramsay is the beautiful mother whom she adored (and who died when she was just thirteen), Mr. Ramsay the brilliant, often tyrannical and demanding father about whom she had mixed feelings; the wonderful Victorian summer house by the sea - so full of life and grace and intensity - the house on the Cornish coast where the Stephen family for many years vacationed. And the poignancy of the book resides in the fact that not only Lily, then, in section three is seeking to recapture this grace which is gone, the beautiful mother and the sunny summer of the past, but Virginia Woolf too, in her own person, as herself, is questing into the past - lamenting, in section two, the gradual, indifferent tides of time which bear it away, striving in section three to recapture it.

HEROINE, MUSE, MOTHER

Every artist, it is said, has in him an autobiographical novel, most often, like James Joyce or D. H. Lawrence, a Bildungsroman-a story of how he came to be what he is-but sometimes, as in Virginia Woolf's case, a portrait of some-one overwhelmingly important person out of the past (her mother), a portrait which, as here, crystallizes other emotions too. Thus Mrs. Ramsay - the strong woman, the beauty, the mother, the heroine; the pivot, like Mrs. Dalloway, of a social wheel; the one, like Clarissa Dalloway, who makes order out of the chaos around her - takes on other meanings too. She becomes, for Lily Briscoe, a kind of muse figure; with her constant matchmaking, her warmth, her sympathy, her great pot of food, she is emblematic of the goodness of life, of nature itself, of the charity of summer which, though so soon swept away by the winds of a colder season, persists and prevails, in memory if not in fact.

SUMMER AND THE SEA

The charity of summer: in a way, just as much as Virginia Woolf's book is about Mrs. Ramsay as a figure of life's goodness, it is about summer itself, about one season of ripeness and, later, the many memories of it. Why is it, after all, that the summers of one's childhood are often so exceptionally meaningful? Why is it that memories of beaches and games by the sea, of faintly shabby country houses, sand heavy towels, wet lawns, wicker chairs (in America, porch swings) and chill night air after the day's heat should have such force? Perhaps because in childhood summer is the great liberator - the time when a child can be alone, responsible only to himself, free, in fact, to confront himself. Perhaps - as especially in Virginia Woolf - because then the family is all together, on vacation from ordinary routines, and free to discover itself as a major reality. Whatever the reason, Virginia Woolf was exceptionally sensitive to the phenomenon: her fascination with the sea, her symbolic use of the beach, blends - in *To the Lighthouse* more than any other of her novels-into a concrete, idyllic evocation of one family's summer, a summer which, like Mrs. Ramsay, provides warmth and meaning enough for the future as well as the past (though we must not forget that the central memory in the minds of Clarissa and Richard Dalloway, Peter Walsh and Sally Seton as well, is also of a summer in the country). But of course besides providing a concrete "background," the recurrent **imagery** of the sea, of the summer and the lighthouse gives further poetic force to the central **themes** of the book, the **themes** of time, of past and present, as the great wonder, the great enigma, and of art as, finally, a way of knowing, of coming to terms with that enigma.

THE SUMMER AND FALL OF SOCIETY

But summer as an idyll - an idyll which must pass-takes on social as well as **metaphysical** significance in *To the Lighthouse,* for the Ramsays' summer in part one may be taken eventually to represent not only the order and innocence of childhood, the warmth of the past, but the order and innocence of pre-war Europe; and the post-war summer ten years later in which nothing and everything have changed may represent post-War Europe. Many historians, in fact, do think of World War I as "the end of an era," the real end, in a sense, of the nineteenth century; and we have seen in *Mrs. Dalloway* that Virginia Woolf herself had strong feelings about the shock and horror of the War, and its influence on the shape and spirit of society. The Ramsays' way of life on their Hebridean island is, after all, a way of life which no longer exists: the elaborate Victorian household-eight children, numerous servants with its calm faith in things, its tableful of sons and daughters and friends and disciples presided over by Mr. Ramsay, the sanguine philosopher who yet imagines he may find his way through the mysterious alphabet of existence, and Mrs. Ramsay, the spirit of beauty with a pot of boeuf en daube-would be archaic, a relic, in a modern world of small families, anxiety, ugliness. Mrs. Woolf's book is thus not only a vision of her own past, but of everybody's-a history not only of her own own but of society's journey from innocence to experience.

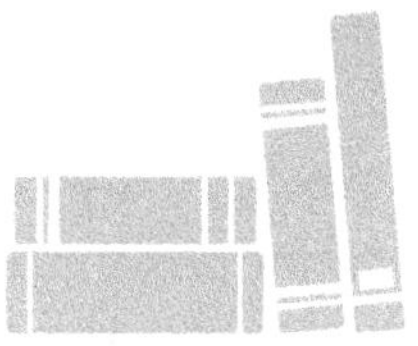

TO THE LIGHTHOUSE

A CRITICAL ANALYSIS

SYMBOLIC DESIGN

As we discussed in the analysis of *Mrs. Dalloway,* Virginia Woolf relies heavily on private symbolism to reveal the inner consciousness of her central characters. In addition, this private symbolism serves an important structural purpose in Mrs. Woolf's art, especially in *To the Lighthouse.* Four outstanding symbols unify the novel and contribute to its meaning: the Lighthouse, the sea, the personality of Mrs. Ramsay, and Lily's painting. In effect, the symbolic design gives coherence to this abstract, evanescent novel's form (indirect interior monologue) and content. Its **themes** center around these symbols.

The meaning of the symbols in *To the Lighthouse* is directly related to Mrs. Woolf's concepts of human values and reality. First of all, she considered that the most important thing about any person is his quest for the meaning of life, and for identification. Personal identity and the means of identification with others are both difficult to perceive and are practically impossible to communicate, according to Virginia Woolf. Each man is invisible to all others, as Lily's painting suggests. Mrs.

Woolf's characters, however, are always searching for reality, aided by small daily illuminations until the moment when she allows them their final insight. They achieve these moments of perception primarily by means of psychic activity. Their private vision of reality is also influenced by their relationships to and interactions with other people. (Mrs. Woolf moves skillfully from mind to mind, as in *Mrs. Dalloway.*)

In a very fundamental way Virginia Woolf's concept of the true meaning and discovery of reality is mystical. Her characters' searches remind us of Eastern mysticism-a mystical quest for cosmic identification. The elusive meaning of the events which bring her characters to their moments of final illumination cannot be described in clear, literal, rational terms. The reader can only feel their meaning, because the writer only suggests it. Reality, in the final analysis, is almost totally abstract; as the critic David Daiches states of *To the Lighthouse,* "experience is seen as something inexpressible yet significant." It is important to bear in mind, therefore, that the interpretation of Virginia Woolf's symbolism is a matter of intuition, just as its creation was.

THE LIGHTHOUSE

As a structural device, it has been suggested by some critics that the Lighthouse symbol penetrates the book to the point where it is reflected in the subdivisions of the novel itself - the three parts of the novel reproducing, in effect, a lighthouse beam with its long flash of light, an interval of darkness, and a short flash. In addition the Lighthouse unifies the **themes** of the opening and closing scenes of the novel, and it also unites the **theme** of James' quest to the symbolism surrounding Lily Briscoe's painting. The reader can also see that the Lighthouse is a symbol for the two opposing attitudes toward life in the Ramsay household, those of Mr. and Mrs. Ramsay.

The symbolism surrounding the Lighthouse is never clearly identified, perhaps because it has a private meaning to each character in the novel. The Lighthouse shifts and changes like reality itself, its nature continually transformed by the context in which it is perceived by each person. It represents, first of all, a quest for values - values which are reflected both in Lily's art and in Mrs. Ramsay's heroic effort to create order out of chaos. The Lighthouse stands apart from the disordered world, shedding light and warmth on it, but it is unable to change anything. Its light reaches and touches the lives of Mr. Ramsay, James and Lily at the close of the novel, only after they set out to reach it. Reaching the Lighthouse seems to signify the establishment of warm, personal relationships with other people (unity as opposed to disorder). Mrs. Ramsay, though dead at the time the Lighthouse is reached, is still present in Lily's thoughts. Her loving, all-pervading presence combines with the flashing light of the Lighthouse (the light of truth and intelligence) to create Lily's moment of final insight. Mrs. Ramsay seems also somehow mystically responsible for the reconciliation of father and son after Mr. Ramsay's warm praise of James. The rocky island, symbol of the harsh reality of the present - death and destiny - stands in sharp contrast to the airy grace of the garden that still survives from the past - the garden Mrs. Ramsay made years before.

THE SEA

This watery symbol is a perfect reflection of the eternal flux and flow of life and time. The sea changes often, at one time a soothing, calming influence, at another time, a savage power of destruction. The sea surrounds the island where the story unfolds (it surrounds the individual and all of mankind) and it surrounds the Lighthouse. And yet, the Lighthouse (man-made) is able to withstand the ravages of the sea (time), thus representing in some sense the uninterrupted continuity of humanity and human values.

MRS. RAMSAY

Mrs. Ramsay is an extraordinarily beautiful woman (like Virginia Woolf's own mother), but she is modest, not arrogant, about her beauty. She cares for material possessions, but gains great pleasure from ordinary, everyday experiences with her family, particularly her children. Her spiritual beauty far surpasses her physical beauty, and-like Cornelia, the legendary Roman widow whose children were her jewels-she is adorned more wonderfully by her eight children and what she had made of them than she could be by any worldly trinkets.

Motherlike - a kind of great earth-mother figure, as well as, with her perfect compassion and beauty, a muse of grace - Mrs. Ramsay's concerns include everyone, friends as well as families, the poor in general (social improvements are her only abstract interest) as well as the pained in particular. But for her own children, she reserves the strongest emotional warmth.

Mr. and Mrs. Ramsay have what is pictured as a good marriage. Lily thinks of them as the symbol of marriage. And yet there is a gulf - a wall of isolation between them, just as there was between the Dalloways, though Virginia Woolf suggests that the Ramsay's marriage is as perfect as a marriage can be. Mrs. Ramsay-who provides her husband with almost superhuman support and encouragement, who lives, indeed, entirely for him and the children, so self-abnegating is she - has never expressed her love directly to her husband. Such intense feeling - the passion at the heart of things - is finally, Mrs. Woolf thinks, inexpressible in words, The loneliness of the individual can only be transcended through actions - through deeds which perfectly communicate feeling and order life - or perhaps through art, which, as it were, objectifies feelings and life. Mr. and Mrs. Ramsay's companionship is perfect, a quiet shared solitude in which implicit love need never be made explicit. Like Clarissa Dalloway, Mrs. Ramsay's outstanding quality is her ability to understand and know people. Unlike Clarissa, however, she has the power to relate to them with a full emotional commitment (at times, perhaps, too full). Like Clarissa again, she forms the still center of peaceful stability, an island of warmth, in the midst of those who scurry and flounder about her, young and old alike. (In an important sense, one can see that Mrs. Ramsay is similar to the Lighthouse in symbolic significance).

Mrs. Ramsay is capable of a kind of love which does not seek to possess and destroy the love object. She seeks to preserve each person's personal identity. (Some critics object that she is a destructive force, an overpowering matriarch, and that the integration of the family is not possible while she is alive. There is little evidence to support this, either in the novel itself or in an examination of Mrs. Woolf's views in her critical works.)

A kind of art of life is Mrs. Ramsay's special creativity, her most distinctive gift. Because of her influence, Mrs. Ramsay's guests relate to one another and become a coherent group. She creates a synthesis indirectly; when she helps her guests to create warm relationships, she hopes to create order out of the disorder and chaos of their silly, spiteful differences of opinion. Mrs. Ramsay tries to destroy strife and unite people in a way that will have lasting significance. This explains her penchant for matchmaking, which influences Paul and Minta. The memory of the moments of love and friendship she is responsible for survive across time, influencing people in subtle but important ways. Thus Mrs. Ramsay's influence has the same permanence as a work of art.

INTUITION VS. REALISM

Mr. and Mrs. Ramsay represent for Virginia Woolf two opposing approaches to life and reality. He is the cynical realist, she has intuitive wisdom and warmth. Mr. Ramsay is a frustrated, somewhat boorish philosopher who considers life hostile. (His disciple, Charles Tansley, echoes his hostility, his narrowness, his dry academic approach to life and his lack of feeling for human values.) Mr. Ramsay's way of helping his children is to make them realistically face the fact that life is harsh and difficult. Consequently, Mr. Ramsay's poverty of spirit is reflected in his lack of warmth. His love, unlike his wife's, is overpowering-he is a tyrannical father and his love for Mrs. Ramsay is one which tries to consume her. He constantly needs her reassurance to sustain his philosophical flights. The antagonism between the domineering father and the son who worships his mother is not without Freudian overtones. (Cam, on the other hand, is more passionately attached to her father, full of mixed but intense feelings, like those of Virginia Woolf for her father.)

In contrast to Mrs. Ramsay's intuitive power to understand life and people, there are numerous hints that Mr. Ramsay is ineffectual and blundering (as when he recites Tennyson's *The Charge of the Light Brigade,* a story of a pathetic blunder). The limitations (and failure) of Mr. Ramsay's thinking and judgment are reflected in the fact that he fragments knowledge in an alphabetic arrangement, lacking the wisdom of an integrated vision of life.

In sum, Mr. Ramsay, the "realist," is a weak, insecure man who needs sympathy and understanding and who has a sterile personality. He is a somewhat pathetic figure in the last section of the novel; he expects sympathy from others, the sympathy his wife had always given to him. He redeems himself somewhat when he breaks down some of the barriers between himself and his son and attempts to communicate with him for the first time.

THE ARTIST

The artistic temperament is presented in the character of Lily Briscoe. Her creativity with ideas and images is constantly compared to Mrs. Ramsay's creativity with people and with life. Both of them seek to order the chaos of existence. Lily's art is eternal, Mrs. Ramsay's influence is eternal. Life and art, Mrs. Woolf seems to be saying, are not so far apart, so distinct, as we might imagine. Though the first seems to be in constant flux while the second is a way of fixing the flux, the chaotic flux itself holds certain perfect moments of stability-moments as artfully created as art itself-which somehow do survive, in memory as well as in art. In a sense, therefore, Mrs. Ramsay's boeuf en daube is as much a work of art as Lily's painting.

Lily adores Mrs. Ramsay but is totally unlike her, lacking not only beauty but also warmth. She is, we come to see, impersonal, withdrawn from life (like so many artists), unable to surrender herself to the vividness and adventure of ordinary experience. Instead, she is an outsider, an observer, who looks on and records-in her painting, her art-her impersonal though passionate vision of the reality in which others participate. Her cool impersonality, her artist's vision, it is suggested, makes her incapable of strong emotional commitment.

But Virginia Woolf finally shows us that - though Mrs. Ramsay seems to embody the very spirit of the earth and human vitality, apparently so far superior to Lily's self-restraint - there is a place for Lily in the scheme of things, as much as for Mrs. Ramsay. For in the end it is Lily, the visionary, who through her painting brings Mrs. Ramsay, the inspirer of paintings, the Muse, the mother, back to life.

LILY'S PAINTING

Virginia Woolf viewed human life as a personal, private quest for some kind of enduring, harmonious reality. In this novel, art represents that reality. Life, in the final analysis, is doomed to be at the mercy of both time and change. Man is mortal, life is transient. Art has the ability to fuse the temporal and the eternal into a form which can enjoy immortality. Mrs. Ramsay, of course, will live beyond the grave too, but only so long as she can live in the memories of those who knew her and loved her. When they are gone, she will fade gradually. Lily's painting has the ability to endure forever.

Poetry, another enduring art form, also plays an important part in the novel. Mr. and Mrs. Ramsay both enjoy poetry immensely. Mr. Carmichael, the poet, appears in the final scene and influences Lily's moment of truth. It is as though he has become an incarnation of the spirit of art and (with his almost sublime indifference even to Mrs. Ramsay, his drugged tolerance) the spirit of fate, or whatever god there may be.

Lily's intuitive vision of truth, symbolized by her ability to finish the painting, is that "reality" is synonymous with harmonious relations-between parents to children, men to women, man and nature, and past and present. The destroyer of "reality" is chaos and people's isolation from one another. Mrs. Ramsay, despite her own shortcomings and difficulties in relationships with people, is the ultimate symbol of vitality, harmony and emotional warmth. When Lily catches this harmony on canvas, it is captured for all time.

Ultimately, however, man is always at the mercy of the destructive forces of time. One can only hope to snatch moments or memories of brief moments of stability and love. All attempts to bring complete order to the chaos of life must fail. But the brief flash of absolute clarity and brief flash of stability, like the short flash of the Lighthouse beam itself, triumph over the eternal flux of time. The assurance of the continued presence of a creative spirit like Mrs. Ramsay's triumphs over the momentary failure of her attempts to create order out of disorder. For example, she failed to help create a perfect marriage for Paul and Minta because of the inflexibility of the materials she was working with. An artist needs the right combination. Both art and life require talent, a talent Mrs. Ramsay had and Minta obviously lacked. Because Lily is an artist, she can do something about what Mrs. Ramsay had discovered about life-give it eternal permanence. This permanence has the ability to transcend the suffering and weakness of mankind, and their final destiny-death.

THE RAVAGES OF TIME

The rather brief middle section of *To the Lighthouse,* entitled "Time Passes," is a poetic tour de force in which the events of ten years seem to be compressed into a single night by the devices of the time-montage. Little by little the house succumbs to the rigors of sea and time. Mrs. Ramsay, the guiding spirit, is gone and reality disintegrates into disorder without her warmth and harmonizing influence. The **theme** is one of decay, destruction and the profusion of darkness, in which people seem powerless against the gradual encroachments of time. Nature and time are totally indifferent to man. Nature's brute force and insensitivity can easily reduce the works of man (the Ramsay house and garden) to a wasteland, if man abandons them for too long. When human vitality is missing, silence, darkness and decay take over. Man is reduced to hopeless insignificance (indicated by the fact that Mrs. Ramsay's death is decreased in importance to a remark in parentheses.) Even divine goodness turns his back, allowing the forces of nature to destroy, because man's penitence, states Virginia Woolf, deserves very little consideration, and his toil deserves only a momentary interval of relief.

It seems that only Mrs. Ramsay could make of the house a living creature-her creation. For she represents everything that has gone from the world-all the lost beauty, the lost warmth and love, the lost possibilities of life. She, who was the spirit of the wonderful Victorian household, the house filled with such a multiplicity, such a variety of energy and grace, somehow embodied the era as well as the family. Mrs. Ramsay was the spirit of the age, a symbol of the serenity and innocence which were possible in those last golden years before the war - the last years of the nineteenth century in a sense - before World War I, the brutal arrival of the twentieth century, shattered that naive late-Romantic dream, that prosperous Victorian calm.

Mrs. McNab, a symbol for man's indestructible spirit, bravely tries to cope with the terrible tide of natural destruction, but the fluidity of ominous darkness (time itself) is too much for her alone. (She reminds us of the cosmic washerwoman whom Joyce envisioned by the Liffey in the Anna Livia Plurabelle section of *Finnegans Wake.*) The corruption and decay are halted only when human vitality returns to the house to stop them, first in the person of Mrs. McNab, then later with the rest of the family and their house guests. The forces of civilization reassert themselves. Mrs. Ramsay, the embodiment of human vitality, is gone, but the positive power of humanity (the power of the human soul) is not stopped by the momentary loss of one person. Life goes on. There is the start of a rebirth as creative energy and human relationships are established in the house again. The rebirth is fully actualized, though only momentarily, when the Lighthouse is reached and the art work captures truth for all eternity.

FUSION OF PROSE AND POETRY

The central portion of *To the Lighthouse,* the interval of darkness entitled "Time Passes," is a beautifully lyrical, poetic passage that is a remarkable demonstration of Mrs. Woolf's ability as a poetic novelist. As we mentioned earlier (in the Introduction to *Mrs. Dalloway*), Virginia Woolf attempted to combine prose and poetry in the hope that the potentialities of both would be maximized. The success of "Time Passes," as an example of this fusion, rests upon an image-filled use of figurative language, one of the characteristic devices of stream-of-consciousness fiction. In this section of the novel, however, the figurative language is primarily descriptive; it is not used to reveal the inner depths of consciousness.

Figurative language-saying one thing in terms of another-does not use words denotatively. It creates meaning by relying upon the **connotations** and associations of words to expand their meanings (figuratively, not literally). This use of language rests on verbal nuance, and subtly lends multiple meanings because of its central ambiguity and because it compresses many ideas and associations into a single word or sentence.

In the previous section, we described the **themes** of this passage-nature's decay and destruction, halted somewhat by the intervention of human energy. These **themes** acquire enormous power, primarily because they are concretized in an unending stream of sense **imagery**, which creates an impressionistic picture of sight, sound and touch. In addition, the use of numerous types of figures of speech heightens the emotional impact of what is perceived, evoking a mood as well as a picture.

In addition to numerous **metaphors** and **similes** concerning darkness and decay, the figure of speech which gives the passage its power is that of personification (attributing human qualities or actions to non-human organisms, inanimate objects or ideas). Thus, darkness, air, light, silence, flowers, loneliness, stillness, the seasons of the year, the Lighthouse, the universe-all have a life of their own. For example, darkness is described with water imagery-it pours down like rain, creates a flood, creeps throughout the house swallowing up things in its path. Similarly, winter holds nights in its hand like a deck of cards, and deals them out regularly. The airs in the house breathe and sigh; the light slides from room to room. Personification gives the death-like stillness a living quality and capacity for motion-a greater forcefulness and potency for destruction than it would have in literal description. When Mrs. Woolf has loneliness and stillness join hands, the effect is chilling.

Nature is more than just alive; she thinks, she chooses courses of action to achieve her mastery over the house built by man, the intruder. At the same time, she is totally insensitive to the human world.

A recurring symbol in this passage is Mrs. Ramsay's shawl, as it gradually loosens and decays. It is a symbol of the warmth which she engendered in others, and it appeared several times in the first section of the novel. After Mrs. Ramsay dies and the house is deserted, the shawl falls to pieces in the period of decay which befalls the house, the family and, symbolically, the twentieth century, when each looses human vitality.

Mrs. Woolf also makes use of other figures of speech such as anastrophe (the deliberate inversion of word order), hidden **alliteration** (not of initial sounds,), anaphora (repetition of a word or phrase at the beginning of clauses or sentences), synecdoche (substitution of a part of something for the whole or the reverse), apostrophe (a thing or person is addressed directly, closely related to personification), periphrasis (circumlocution), and hyperbole (overstatement, exaggeration).

An impressionistic use of **imagery** and symbolism in literature can have a powerful effect, because it can evoke a mood which delights the senses, as we have demonstrated in "Time Passes." Its effect is primarily emotional-recording the emotional reactions of the characters in the novel or evoking a response from the reader. Poetic fiction, as a technique used exclusively, however, has numerous drawbacks. It leads to a novel which may suggest many meanings, while clarifying few of them. It may delight our senses, but a novel which relies more on reaction than action lacks both plot and the conflicts of will that an action-oriented novel makes possible; that is, for all its exquisite beauty of **imagery**, it lacks substance because it is too subjective. Impressions of events can never be as powerful or vital as the events themselves. Impressionistic **imagery** is most successful as a supplement to the action and description of a narrative, not as a substitute for it.

TO THE LIGHTHOUSE

CHARACTER ANALYSES

MRS. RAMSAY

A beautiful and loving woman, Mrs. Ramsay is - and represents - all that is good in the world. Indeed, she seems sometimes to be almost too perfect. She is, first of all, a perfect mother, and her children, of course, adore her. Second, she is - obviously - a perfect wife, one who gives her husband all the support and reassurance he could possibly need; he is full of insecurity, must constantly be told that he is worthwhile, that his work is good, that she is behind him; she is full of strength and love and courage, which flow into him, enabling him to go on. Third, she is in a sense in which Clarissa never is, "the perfect hostess." Mrs. Ramsay seems to cast a net of warmth and love over the isolated individuals at her dinner table, bringing a kind of wonderful social coherence out of the chaos that might otherwise have engulfed everyone. Fourth, she is a perfect woman - not just because she is a mother, a wife, a hostess, but also because she is a kind of embodiment of the feminine principle, the life principle, the principle of affirmation. The marriage she advocates to Lily is really a marriage to the world, a feast of life. Fifth, because she is beautiful and courageous, wise and gay, Mrs. Ramsay is a kind of muse-figure, and also a kind of heroine; she is, that is, both a doer of great things (because life is itself a kind of great deed for her) and, more, an inspirer of great things, not only in her husband but in the artist, Lily Briscoe, whose final vision of life is in a sense granted by Mrs. Ramsay. Thus, heroine, muse, mother and more, Mrs. Ramsay seems almost too perfect, "too much," as one critic has noted. Yet for most readers she is drawn with such liveliness and so much love that she comes vividly to life despite what might in the hands of another novelist be an impossible flawlessness. It is Virginia Woolf's - and Lily Briscoe's and Charles Tansley's and Mr. Ramsay's and James' and everyone else's - impressions of her that we are being given, after all, a subjective though many-sided portrait, and not an objective case history.

MR. RAMSAY

Where Mrs. Ramsay is completely self-abnegating, outward-turning, subjective, feminine, Mr. Ramsay is a kind of embodiment of the masculine principle: self-centered, objective, melodramatic, needing constant love and reassurance and sympathy. He is a philosopher, a famous one apparently, for students and disciples have followed him even to his summer home, where he is, as always, engaged in a kind of search for reality, an attempt to get through the "alphabet" of existence and define for himself all the terms of life. Though he is at first an irritating figure and perhaps even, at times, an almost comical figure, by the end of the book he becomes partly pathetic and partly heroic.

CHARLES TANSLEY

A rather unpleasant, ambitious young man, dry, scholarly, academic, Charles Tansley feels keenly his social "inferiority" to the Ramsays and their friends. He admires Mr. Ramsay as a philosopher, and the beautiful Mrs. Ramsay, but he wants most of all to prove himself their equal.

LILY BRISCOE

Lily Briscoe is a good friend and protegee of Mrs. Ramsay's, though it is doubtful that Mrs. Ramsay understands anything of Lily's mind or art. Shy, sensitive, reserved, virginal, Lily fears marriage and emotional involvement; she wants to keep herself aloof, pure, for she is totally dedicated to her art. At first it seems as though Lily is wrong to feel this way, as though she ought to take Mrs. Ramsay's advice and marry at once, for otherwise she will miss all the goodness of life. But in the end we see that Lily too, has her function, for it is she - through her art - as it were, who resurrects and immortalizes the beautiful Mrs. Ramsay; just as the artist must depend on the muse, after all, the muse must depend on the artist.

WILLIAM BANKES

A widower and a scientist, Mr. Bankes is superficially rather like Lily-reserved, orderly, a little cold. He is more than half in love with Mrs. Ramsay, as most men are. Though he seems something like Lily, in addition, we should note that basically William Bankes is very different from Lily, for he lacks her creativity, her artist's gift of life which, in its way, is almost the equivalent of Mrs. Ramsay's gift.

AUGUSTUS CARMICHAEL

An elderly friend of Mr. Ramsay's, Augustus Carmichael is heavy, calm, seemingly indifferent to Mrs. Ramsay - the only man, indeed, who is so indifferent to her charm and beauty. He is, we come to see, a kind of fate-figure, indifferent to the poignancy and beauty of particular individuals.

PAUL RAYLEY AND MINTA DOYLE

This young couple are healthy, attractive, energetic, and not quite worth Mrs. Ramsay's efforts. Though Paul is an honest, forthright, well-intentioned and rather stupid young man, passionately in love with his wife, Minta, in particular, tends to be a little flighty, a little superficial. She lacks back-bone, as Mrs. Ramsay herself sees; she lacks the special quality, the special individuality, which Lily has, for instance. Nevertheless, the love which transfigures this pair is an important part of the magic of Mrs. Ramsay's party, an important part, in a sense, of the spell which Mrs. Ramsay has cast on all those who are privileged to sit around her table.

ANDREW, PRUE, NANCY, ROSE, JASPER, CAM, JAMES, ETC.

None of the Ramsay children are very clearly differentiated in the first part of the book, though Cam and James become more distinctly individuals at the close of the novel.

MRS. MCNAB

Mrs. McNab is the old cleaning-woman, who plays such an important role in section two of the book. She becomes, like the washerwomen in *Finnegans Wake*, a symbol of, among other things, the frail but indefatigable spirit which-muttering, grotesque, full of complaints-nevertheless persists, whenever possible (like Lily, the artist) in redeeming its most precious possessions, its memories, from oblivion.

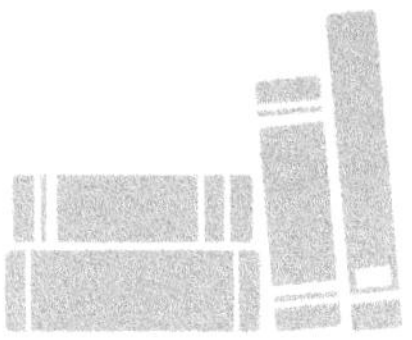

VIRGINIA WOOLF

CRITICAL COMMENTARY

FIRST REACTIONS AND SECOND THOUGHTS

Virginia Woolf's secure position as a member of the "Bloomsbury Group" - in a way she was just as much as hub of her own social circle as Clarissa Dalloway and Mrs. Ramsay are of theirs-assured her informed admiration and good reviews almost from the start of her career. She was dazzling enough from the first too, so that even outside Bloomsbury her work found immediate and enthusiastic approval. After a while, however, her identification with Bloomsbury became a liability as well as an asset: the growing anti-Bloomsbury movement - a groundswell of reaction against what seemed (and often was) the narrow snobbishness and sterile aestheticism of this group of establishment intellectuals - began with D. H. Lawrence and later included the entire iconoclastic Scrutiny group (many of them passionate Lawrentians), led by the influential critic F. R. Leavis. This movement attacked Mrs. Woolf for the very Bloomsbury traits which had impressed so many other readers-her elegance and delicacy of style, her poetic impressionism, her carefully limited subject matter, her deliberate subjectivity.

ANTI-BLOOMSBURY VOICES

A good example of the kind of attacks which the anti-Bloomsbury Scrutiny critics made on Mrs. Woolf is W. H. Mellers' review of *The Years,* in which the critic went on to discuss the novelist's faults in general, as well as those of *The Years* in particular (cf. Selected Bibliography). Like Dr. Leavis, Mellers finds that *To the Lighthouse* is Mrs. Woolf's only really successful book, and then he declares that "When she had written *To the Lighthouse* there were three courses open to Mrs. Woolf. Either she could enlarge her scope, do something fresh; or she could stop writing altogether; or she could cheat by way of technique. She chose the last of these alternatives. In *The Waves* there is a fatal falsification between what her impressions actually are and what they are supposed to signify - they are pinned to her prose like so many dead butterflies. Mrs. Woolf goes through the appropriate gestures (doors open, doors shut), uses the appropriate formulae (the rose blossoms, the petal falls), but the champing beast on the shore confesses itself a mechanical toy, and the artificially artful parallel with the waves hardly pretends to be anything more than a parallel. The artfulness of the method makes the immediacy and hence the quality of the impressions themselves deteriorate ... essentially," he adds, Mrs. Woolf's "attitude is that of the under-graduate - or Bloomsbury-poet."

Later Mr. Mellers goes on to discuss what seems to him the "purposelessness" of *The Waves,* which he seems to couple with what he regards as Mrs. Woolf's over - "refinement." Like the Leavises, of course, he is writing out of a morally oriented critical tradition, a tradition (for by now it is that) which values books insofar as they are "mature" and socially conscious. Thus he concludes that "to speak of Mrs. Woolf's refinement reminds us of her celebrated femininity, which quality seems to go hand in hand with the curiously tepid Bloomsbury prose into which she has always, in unguarded moments been inclined to trickle. Here, anyway, it only enforces the feeling of weakness and sterility, and one can but reflect dismally on the inanity of a world in which the only positives seem to be 'silence and solitude.' These incoherently reminiscent mumblings seem purposely to ignore the human will and all it entails...."

In a more personal attack on Mrs. Woolf, (though it is hard to see how anyone could be much more personal than Mellers), Queenie Leavis, Dr. Leavis' wife discusses the novelist's feminism in greater detail, within the framework of a review of the feminist tract *Three Guineas*, which Mrs. Woolf published in 1938. Of course Mrs. Leavis - not by birth a member of the upper-class intellectual aristocracy (as Mrs. Woolf was) - is immediately put off by Mrs. Woolf's declaration that the book is aimed at "women of our class," meaning women whose "fathers function at Westminster, who 'spend vast sums annually upon party funds; upon sport; upon grouse moors ...,'" etc. Indeed, this statement of Mrs. Woolf's, plus what is apparently a personal resentment (and a rather understandable one) of the hereditary privileges-financial and professional-of Bloomsbury, leads Mrs. Leavis to assert that "It is no use attempting to discuss the book for what it claims to be, which is a sort of chatty restatement of the rights and wrongs of women of Mrs. Woolf's class, with occasional reflections, where convenient, on the wrongs of other kinds of Englishwomen." It is "no use' apparently because "Mrs. Woolf, by her own account, has personally received considerably more in the way of economic ease than she is humanly entitled to and, as this book reveals, has enjoyed the equally relaxing ease of an uncritical (not to say flattering) social circle: she cannot be supposed to have suffered any worse injury from mankind than a rare unfavorable review. Writing this book was evidently a form of self-indulgence-altruism exhibits a different tone, it is not bad-tempered, peevishly sarcastic, and incoherent as this book is throughout. As a reviewer I must say it impresses me as unpleasant self-indulgence, and as a member of a class of educated women Mrs. Woolf has apparently never heard of [educated women from the lower and middle classes] I feel entitled to add it is also highly undesirable."

Of course, Mrs. Woolf brought much of this savage hostility down on her own head by her (apparently) ignorant and careless statements about "our class," and of course, Mrs. Leavis is perfectly justified, for this reason, in feeling personal resentment. On the other hand, it should be added that Mrs. Leavis' reaction to Mrs. Woolf-like much of the anti-Bloomsbury feeling among the Scrutiny group-seems to be almost wholly personal, almost wholly without much intellectual justification. Certainly "Caterpillars of the Commonwealth Unite!" as Mrs. Leavis' review is fancifully entitled, itself exhibits at least as much bad-temper, peevish sarcasm and incoherence as its author accuses Mrs. Woolf of indulging in. For more balanced appraisals of Virginia Woolf's achievement, then, we will have to go to critics who feel less personal emotional involvement with their subject, either because they are of a different generation or because they have somehow managed to transcend the class consciousness which seems to be so much more intense in England than in America.

PRO VIRGINIA WOOLF

A. D. Moody, for instance, whose Evergreen Pilot book Virginia Woolf provides a useful and thorough introduction to the novelist, is an Englishman who seems to be of a different generation (if not literally then spiritually) from the Leavises, Mellers, etc. He resists, for example, the easy temptation immediately and completely to identify Virginia Woolf with Bloomsbury. "From the first," he notes, "not sharing the Bloomsbury complacency, and being above its narrowness, she had seen the inadequacy of its ideal of a civilization merely in the mind. Rachel Vinrace rejects Hirst on precisely those grounds, demanding not merely to contemplate but really to feel things, to live wholly, from the deepest sources of her being outwards through the mind, and into personal and social relationships. This demand gave Virginia Woolf a perspective in which to place the achievement of the mind alone against other kinds of human achievement, so that she could celebrate its vital function without ignoring, as Bloomsbury did, that it would be monstrous and ineffectual on its own." Furthermore, he adds, that though Mrs. Woolf's "own experience of life was relatively very limited" she "made the utmost of the life she did know by preserving, in her rendering of it, a clear and positive awareness of other forms of life which were valuable. She was thus able to view her own world with a poised impersonality, and to comprehend its place and value within the whole of which it was a part."

Other lucid and impartial judges of Mrs. Woolf's achievement have included, over the years, such major critics as Leon Edel and Erich Auerbach, in a carefully documented chapter of his famous Mimesis (cf. Bibliography) places Mrs. Woolf's *To the Lighthouse* at the end of a long chain of great literary works (beginning with the *Odyssey* and progressing through the *Inferno, Hamlet, Madame Bovary,* etc.) as the most modern example - the most recent stage in the evolution-of western literary techniques for depicting the nature of reality. Finally he concluded that *To the Lighthouse* "is one of the few books of this type [he compares it to *Ulysses,* for instance] which are filled with good and genuine love but also, in its feminine way, with irony, amorphous sadness, and doubt of life. Yet what realistic depth is achieved in every individual occurrence, for example the measuring of the stocking!"

Leon Edel similarly attempts to place Mrs. Woolf's work in a larger tradition, in his case not the whole tradition of western literature but rather the uniquely contemporary tradition of the subjective or "psychological" novel. And his final balanced appraisal of the author's achievement is probably the most perceptive of the critical conclusions discussed here. Like Mellers, he notes the curiously undifferentiated, unindividualized quality of the streams of consciousness which Mrs. Woolf records; everyone in a Virginia Woolf novel seems to think in the same kind of poetic prose; there is no attempt to distinguish between particular characters. On the other hand, unlike Mellers and like Mrs. Woolf's keenest enthusiasts, Edel is able to appreciate the quality of this poetic prose, its brilliance as poetry. Mrs. Woolf, he writes, "achieves a remarkable, shimmering effect of experience. Light, tone, colour play through her cadenced works in a constant search for mood and with no attempt to impart an individual character to the style of thought. There is no attempt at portrait painting; rather does shy try to evoke a state of feeling by a kind of mental poesy. The same vein of poetry runs through all the minds she creates for us. It is as if she had created a single device or **convention**, to be applied universally, in the knowledge that the delicacy of the perception, the waves of feeling, will wash over her readers as she washes them over her characters. This is alike her achievement and its fatal flaw. The bright flame-like vividness of her books creates beautiful illuminated surfaces. There is no tragic depth in them, only the pathos of things lost and outlived, the past irretrievable or retrieved as an ache in the present."

There have been, of course, a number of thorough and for the most part perceptive full-length studies of Mrs. Woolf's life and works. These include works by Joan Bennett, Monique Nathan, A. D. Moody, Dorothy Brewster, David Daiches, and others (cf. Bibliography). A reasonably good recent book of this type is Dorothy Brewster's Virginia Woolf, a work which considers Mrs. Woolf as a critic as well as as a novelist, and which in several cases attempts to refute the most violently anti-Bloomsbury attacks on her. "Her very genius singles her out for attack," she points out. But, indeed, we should remember that even if a critic like W. H. Mellers is right in calling Mrs. Woolf "only a very minor sort of poet," we have not got so many poets in any rank of society that we can afford to ignore or overlook or deprecate the achievements of even the most minor ones.

VIRGINIA WOOLF

ESSAY QUESTIONS AND ANSWERS

Question: How does Virginia Woolf make use of time in her novels?

Answer: Virginia Woolf uses time in many different ways in her novels. First of all, of course, she has written novels (especially her earlier ones) in which time passes normally, its progress undistorted and "natural." A novel like *The Voyage Out,* for instance, makes use of a reasonably conventional time-scheme, day succeeding day in ordinary, undramatic fashion. With *Jacob's Room,* however, which illuminates only certain highlights-intensely important moments-in time, Virginia Woolf began to distort her time-schemes to serve literary or **metaphysical** purposes. In doing this she was, as we've seen (cf. General Introduction and Introductions to *Mrs. Dalloway* and *To the Lighthouse*), influenced by two separate but interrelated literary and intellectual trends. One was the trend toward subjectivity, the trend which eventually produced novels of subjectivity or "psychological" novels like those of Joyce, Proust and Dorothy Richardson as well as those of Mrs. Woolf. These works distorted time in order to present it from the subjective point of view of the individual experiencing it, rather than from an objective or "scientific" point of view.

The second trend was the related tendency of Bergson and other thinkers to conceive of time solely in terms of subjective experience. Such thinkers declared, in other words, that time is only real as a record of individual duration - la duree - and that all chronology is therefore the chronology of subjectivity, involving mainly the relationship between past and future (the present having thus no existence except as a single moment during which past relentlessly "gnaws" into future).

In a work like *Mrs. Dalloway,* then, Virginia Woolf depicted her heroine and those around her living at least as intensely in the past as in the present. In *To the Lighthouse* Mrs. Woolf also produced a distorted time-scheme, one even more obviously distorted than that of *Mrs. Dalloway.* The first part takes place on the afternoon of a summer day before World War I; the second part seems at once like the passage of a single night and the passage of ten years; the third part is the morning of the "next" day-a day actually ten years after Part I. Again, in *Orlando* and *The Waves,* Mrs. Woolf's chronologies were unconventional: *Orlando* relates the history of a single man-woman who, over a period of four hundred years, has become thirty-eight years old; *The Waves* sets the lives of six friends against the rising and setting of the sun on a single summer day at the beach (there is, of course, an obvious **metaphor** being made). Even *The Years,* a more conventional, later novel, deals with isolated moments or periods in the lives of three generations of the Pargiter family; its chronology spans about seventy years.

Question: Why has Virginia Woolf been considered a writer of symbolic novels?

Answer: Although the original French "symbolistes" were poets, Virginia Woolf, a poetic novelist, has often, with good reason, been considered a true symbolist, for throughout her work she uses objects and even people-as did the symbolists - not only to represent themselves but to suggest some larger theme or idea or feeling. In *Mrs. Dalloway,* for instance, the implicit relationship between Septimus Warren Smith and Clarissa Dalloway serves not only dramatic but also (and mainly) thematic (or, as we have said, **metaphysical**) purposes. Septimus is Clarissa's "dark double," an example of the way in which the insane view the world the sane have made (and, it may be noted, he sees with the often paradoxically clear eyes of madness.) Also in *Mrs. Dalloway* the motorcar which Clarissa, Septimus and others see in Bond Street serves as a symbol both of England's majesty and of death. Other symbols in *Mrs. Dalloway* include the nurse in the park, the skywriting airplane, Doris Kilman, Sir William Bradshaw, the old lady at the window, and even Clarissa's party.

To the Lighthouse, of course, also employs a good deal of symbolism. Mrs. Ramsay, for instance, is not only herself, perhaps the major character in the book; she also represents all the beautiful potentialities of what we might call the feminine principle: she is heroine, muse, mother, almost a personification of the life-force. Mr. Ramsay, on the other hand, represents the masculine principle: questing, uncompromising, egotistical. Lily Briscoe, of course, represents the artist and all the potentialities as well as the problems of art. Even old Augustus Carmichael becomes at the end a kind of fate-figure. Objects which take on symbolic importance include the pot of boeuf en daube, the Lighthouse itself, the sea and Lily's painting.

Orlando and *The Waves,* as well as Mrs. Woolf's other novels, are also, of course, full of symbolism. One of the most obvious examples might be the character Percival in *The Waves,* who is never seen but often spoken of. He seems to represent-like the medieval hero (Perceval or Parsifal) for whom he is named-all that is pure and good in the world, a kind of heroic ideal. And, as noted earlier, the waves and sun on the beach, when juxtaposed with the histories of the six narrators, make, symbolically or metaphorically, an important philosophical point about the nature of man's life on this earth.

BIBLIOGRAPHY

WORKS BY VIRGINIA WOOLF

Novels

The Voyage Out. London (Hogarth Press) 1915. New York (Harcourt, Brace) 1920 (a revised text which has not been published in England).

Night and Day. London (Hogarth Press) 1919. New York (Harcourt, Brace) 1920.

Jacob's Room. London (Hogarth Press) 1922. New York (Harcourt, Brace) 1923. Available in paperback.

Mrs. Dalloway. London (Hogarth Press) 1925. New York (Harcourt, Brace) 1925. Available in paperback.

To the Lighthouse. London (Hogarth Press) 1927. New York (Harcourt, Brace) 1927. Available in an inexpensive edition.

The Waves. London (Hogarth Press) 1931. New York (Harcourt, Brace) 1931. Available in paperback.

The Years. London (Hogarth Press) 1937. New York (Harcourt, Brace) 1937.

Between the Acts. London (Hogarth Press) 1941. New York (Harcourt, Brace) 1941.

Other Fiction

Monday or Tuesday. Richmond (Hogarth Press) 1921. New York (Harcourt, Brace) 1921. (Incorporated *The Mark on the Wall* 1917, and *Kew Gardens* 1919, issued from the original Hogarth Press; and printed six other stories or sketches.)

Orlando: a Biography. London (Hogarth Press) 1928. New York (Harcourt, Brace) 1928. Available in paperback.

Flush: a Biography. London (Hogarth Press) 1933. New York (Harcourt, Brace) 1933.

A Haunted House and Other Stories. London (Hogarth Press) 1943. New York (Harcourt, Brace) 1944. (Incorporates most of *Monday or Tuesday* and includes twelve other stories.)

Essays And Other Writings

The Common Reader: First Series. London (Hogarth Press) 1925. New York (Harcourt, Brace) 1925. Available in paperback.

A Room of One's Own. London (Hogarth Press) 1929. New York (Harcourt, Brace) 1929. Available in paperback.

The Common Reader: Second Series. London (Hogarth Press) 1932. New York (Harcourt, Brace) 1932. Available in paperback.

Three Guineas. London (Hogarth Press) 1938. New York (Harcourt, Brace) 1938.

Roger Fry: a Biography. London (Hogarth Press) 1940. New York (Harcourt, Brace) 1940.

The Death of the Moth and Other Essays. London (Hogarth Press) 1942. New York (Harcourt, Brace) 1942. Available in paperback.

The Moment and Other Essays. London (Hogarth Press) 1947. New York (Harcourt, Brace) 1948.

The Captain's Death Bed and Other Essays. London (Hogarth Press) 1950. New York (Harcourt, Brace) 1950.

A Writer's Diary. Edited by Leonard Woolf. London (Hogarth Press) 1953. New York (Harcourt, Brace) 1954.

Virginia Woolf and Lytton Strachey: Letters. Edited by Leonard Woolf and James Strachey. London (Hogarth Press) 1956. New York (Harcourt, Brace) 1956.

SELECTED WORKS ABOUT VIRGINIA WOOLF (BOOKS AND ARTICLES)

Auerbach, Erich. *Mimesis: The Representation of Reality in Western Literature,* chapter XX. Princeton, 1953. Available in paperback. A thorough and useful study of Mrs. Woolf's "representational" method in *To the Lighthouse.*

Beach, J. W. "Virginia Woolf," *English Journal* XXVI, 1937, pp. 603-612.

Beck, Warren. "For Virginia Woolf," *Forms of Modern Fiction,* ed. W. V. O'Connor. Minneapolis, 1948, pp. 229-239.

Bennett, Joan. *Virginia Woolf: Her Art as a Novelist.* Cambridge and New York, 1945.

Brace, Marjorie. "Worshipping Solid Objects: the Pagan World of Virginia Woolf," *Accent Anthology,* ed. Quinn and Shattuck. New York, 1946, pp. 489-495.

Bradbrook, M. C. "Notes on the Style of Mrs. Woolf," *Scrutiny* I, 1932, pp. 33-38.

Brewster, Dorothy. *Virginia Woolf.* New York, 1962. A brief but reasonably thorough life-and-works study which deals with Virginia Woolf's contributions as a critic as well as with her major fiction.

______. Virginia Woolf's London. *New York, 1960.*

Brower, R. A. "Something Central which Permeated: Virginia Woolf and *Mrs. Dalloway," The Fields of Light.* New York, 1951, pp. 123-137.

Chambers, R. L. *The Novels of Virginia Woolf.* Edinburgh, 1947.

Daiches, David. *Virginia Woolf.* Norfolk, Connecticut, 1942.

Delattre, F. Le *Roman psychologique de Virginia Woolf.* Paris, 1932. Contains an interesting discussion of "la duree bergsonienne."

Edel, Leon. *The Modern Psychological Novel.* New York, 1955. A brilliant, lucidly written study of the form in which Mrs. Woolf, along with James, Joyce, Proust and a few others, was a trail-blazer. Available in paperback.

Empson, William. "Virginia Woolf," *Scrutinies* Vol. II, ed. E. Rickword. London, 1931, pp. 203-216.

Forster, E. M. *Virginia Woolf: The Rede Lecture.* Cambridge and New York, 1942. Views on Virginia Woolf by her most distinguished Bloomsbury contemporary.

Graham, John. "Time in the Novels of Virginia Woolf," *University of Toronto Quarterly*, XVII, 1949, pp. 186-201.

Hafley, James. *The Glass Roof: Virginia Woolf as Novelist.* California, 1954. Includes a useful list of foreign reviews and criticism.

Hartman, G. H. "Virginia's Web," *Chicago Review,* XIII, 1960, pp. 20-32.

Holtby, Winifred. *Virginia Woolf.* London, 1932.

Horizon, May and June, 1941. Articles by T. S. Eliot, Duncan Grant, Rose Macaulay, William Plomer, and V. Sackville-West.

Isherwood, Christopher. "Virginia Woolf," *Decision,* May, 1941.

Johnstone, J. K. *The Bloomsbury Group. A study of E. M. Forster, Lytton Strachey, Virginia Woolf, and their circle.* London, 1954. Contains a long and detailed chapter on Mrs. Woolf's major novels, and relates them to the Bloomsbury habit of mind.

Leavis, F. R. "After *To the Lighthouse,*" *Scrutiny,* X, 1942. pp. 295-298. A discussion of Mrs. Woolf's work by the leading British critic who has become one of her (and Bloomsbury's) chief antagonists.

Leavis, Q. D. "Caterpillars of the Commonwealth Unite!" *Scrutiny,* VII, 1938. Reprinted in *The Importance of Scrutiny,* ed. Eric Bentley. New York, 1948. A bitter attack on Mrs. Woolf's particular brand of feminism by Dr. Leavis' wife, who, however, proposes no sensible alternative of her own.

Mellers, W. H. "Mrs. Woolf and Life," *Scrutiny*, VI, 1937, pp. 71-75. Also reprinted in *The Importance of Scrutiny* (see above). Another anti-Bloomsbury outburst which provides useful insights into Mrs. Woolf's faults as a novelist and thinker.

Moody, A. D. *Virginia Woolf.* New York and Edinburgh, 1963. An Evergreen Pilot Book. A brief and useful study of Mrs. Woolf's life-and-works. (Paperback.)

Nathan, Monique. *Virginia Woolf.* New York, 1961. An Evergreen Profile Book. Less thorough and complete than Moody's study, but containing a number of photographs of people and places that were important in V.W.'s life, plus a short anthology of her writings. (Paperback.)

Pippett, Aileen. *The Moth and the Star: A Biography of Virginia Woolf.* Boston, 1955. Contains extensive quotations from Virginia Woolf's letters to V. Sackville-West over the period from 1922 to 1941, and is the *only* full biography to have been written of Mrs. Woolf so far. Available in paperback.

Troy, William. "Virginia Woolf: The Novel of Sensibility," *Literary Opinion in America*, ed. M. D. Zabel. New York, 1951, pp. 324-337.

www.ingramcontent.com/pod-product-compliance
Lightning Source LLC
Chambersburg PA
CBHW070035130125
20264CB00016BA/1504

9781645425267